# TO MY SISTERS IN CHRIST

*To My Sisters in Christ*

**Copyright © 2020 by John A. Crawford**

All rights reserved.

No part of this book may be reproduced in any form or by any electronic or mechanical means, including information storage and retrieval systems, without written permission from the author, except for the use of brief quotations in a book review.

> All scriptures taken from the New King James Version®. Copyright © 1982 by Thomas Nelson. Used by permission. All rights reserved.
>
> Scripture quotations taken from the Amplified® Bible (AMPC), Copyright © 1954, 1958, 1962, 1964, 1965, 1987 by The Lockman Foundation Used by permission. www.lockman.org

ISBN: 979-8-3485-3062-4

*A Publication of Tall Pine Books*

|| *tallpinebooks.com*

*Published in the United States of America

# TO MY SISTERS IN CHRIST

### JOHN A. CRAWFORD

*To God.*

*He never leaves me or forsakes me. Gave me all that I have. Has been a friend that has been closer than a brother. He has kept all his promises.*

# CONTENTS

| | |
|---|---:|
| Introduction | ix |
| 1. Good Girls Like Bad Boys | 1 |
| 2. He Won't Open Up to Me | 19 |
| 3. Communication | 37 |
| 4. Honor | 53 |
| 5. Come Out from Among Them | 71 |
| 6. Manage Your Emotions | 89 |
| 7. Impress | 105 |
| 8. Don't Come Against Him | 121 |
| 9. Different Cultures | 135 |
| About the Author | 147 |
| Resources | 149 |

# INTRODUCTION

Throughout time, challenges have been seen that are encountered in relationships. The challenges can be seen all around us in many areas. The impacts that occur in the relationships affect so many others. This often takes place without being noticed until so much damage has been done that the relationship seems beyond remedy . It's not just in one community or one ethnic group. It can be seen in every community or ethnic group across the board.

Fault finding and finger pointing is not the recipe to get things resolved—not to say that there is a quick fix that will make everything better overnight. A person cannot take a pill, cry themselves to sleep, and have everything resolved in the morning. They won't be able to run some software on the computer and look to the program to fix all the problems. One good place to start would be the Word of God. Things can take time. We can look at what steps we can take.

How can better relationships take place? The hot topic would be with the relationship between women and men on the course to be married. Has it ever been considered what occurs beyond this relationship and what it will become?

Past hurts can turn into roots of bitterness. Bad experiences turn out to be judgments that are brought on others. The innocent can be contaminated with the effects of the hurts and bitterness and are unaware. A person could be smiling one minute, and the next, their arms are crossed because now they are upset.

Many can turn to advice of friends. The wrong music to calm themselves. Shopping to build self-esteem from depression. Even turn to habits that will take them down the wrong road such as clubs, alcohol, drugs, and the wrong company. The person can find themselves more upset than before they turned to these different vices. Unfortunately, this process can start at an earlier age than suspected. As it has been said, "Looking for love in all the wrong places."

To answer the question on how to get better relationships to take place would be to turn to the strong foundation: the Word of God. In the middle of the frustration and chaos, it is the last thing that a lot of people would think about, but it should be the first. You may be surprised to see how the Word can address your situation. The real results will come when you are in a relationship with God. Wouldn't it be great to avoid the issues? Prevention would be a great method.

I would like to think about this book as a love letter from your brother in Christ. As if I were sitting down with a group of sisters in Christ and sharing on some items that may not usually be discussed. Thinking on the feedback received from men and women in the past while going through their challenges. Seeing the impact on the children, family, and friends. Everyone cannot sit back and say that every issue and every problem is the man. There are some things we can take a hard and honest look. Some of the things that are brought up may not be comfortable to talk about. Some may be on the edge. Some may be offensive. Some things may make you mad. I would encourage you to read this letter until the end.

You may have to put the letter down because you are upset; however, you can come back to it later and continue. My heart is for your God-given desires to come to pass in your life and for you to be able to receive them and keep them. My heart is for you to do better and have better and not be deceived. No matter where you are in life. If you are in a bad state in your life, it can be good. If you are doing good, then become great. Everyone can grow.

In reading the chapters of the letter, it would be best to be able to read with understanding. If you have not received Jesus Christ into your heart, I would encourage you to do so now. If you have in the past and have gotten away from God, I encourage you to recommit your life to Him once again. It would be a great thing for you and give you understanding as you read the content of this letter. There is not judgment here. I want to help you to be able to read with understanding and help your spiritual needs to be met.

## ACCORDING TO SCRIPTURE:

> That if you confess with your mouth the Lord Jesus and believe in your heart that God has raised Him from the dead, you will be saved. For with the heart one believes unto righteousness, and with the mouth confession is made unto salvation. (Romans 10:9-10)

This can be done in prayer. Invite Jesus Christ into your heart. Believe that He is the Son of God and that God has raised Him from the dead. Confess Jesus Christ as Lord.

## SAY THIS PRAYER:

> I am a sinner; I need a Savior. I need Jesus. I turn from sin, and I turn to You. I believe in my heart that You raised Jesus from the dead, and I ask Jesus now to come into my heart and be the Lord of my life. I receive Him now as Lord of my life, and I confess with my mouth that Jesus is Lord! Thank You for my salvation! In Jesus' name, amen.

Now that this has been done, you will have a better understanding of what you are about to read.

## ACCORDING TO SCRIPTURE:

And He said, "To you it has been given to know the mysteries of the kingdom of God, but to the rest *it is given* in parables, that 'Seeing they may not see, And hearing they may not understand.'" (Luke 8:10)

Ready. Set. Let's GO!

# 1
## GOOD GIRLS LIKE BAD BOYS

This has been a phrase that we hear time and time again. When the good girl is seen with the bad boy, everyone would look at the nice young lady and wonder why she is with this person. Is there a self-esteem problem? Is it because the person is popular? Is she worried about what people think of her?

It is one thing if the person is making a change in their life. It's totally different if they have no respect or regard for the good girl and she is still with them. Do not try to change the person. Let God be the influence. You do not have to be His special agent. The girl's parents will try to intervene. The good girl can have many good boys all around her, but they go unseen. I'm saying "good *boy*" because of the young age that this normally occurs.

The good boys wonder what the good girl would see in the bad boys. Good boys don't seem to stand a chance. Some women that are reading this now are reflecting on the past. Keep in mind, it is the past. Look at where some seeds may have been planted. The hurt from the bad boys can be brought into future relationships and to those that are involved in that relationship.

It will be especially important that forgiveness has taken place regarding past relationships. <u>Forgiveness</u> is not a curse word. It may feel like one right now. Healing needs to take place from the bad boy before starting a new relationship with the <u>godly man</u>. Forgiveness helps you. Forgiveness is not a feeling. It is a choice. You may not feel like it, but you can choose to forgive and act on it until your feelings get in line with your choice. When you forgive, you are not bringing it back up again, you are not rehearsing the issue time and time again, you are not rolling your eyes or giving the person the cold shoulder. In fact, you will speak to the person when you see them in public. No gossip behind the person's back. Lose the attitude and speak to the person in a tone that you would like for someone to speak to you. I needed to make it clear on what forgiveness includes. When it is a choice, you will continue to do the right thing until your feelings line up with your actions. This will truly give God something to work with when He is working on your behalf, because your heart will be right.

If you do not forgive, you are watering the root of bitterness. Forgiveness kills that root and gives your heart good ground for the next relationship. This will give you a pure approach going forward. More importantly, this will prevent you from poisoning others. No one likes the wrong roots or weeds in their garden in the natural. The natural garden is temporary. The matters of the heart last a lot longer. God's Word says for you to guard your heart, because out of it springs the issues of life. This will affect your destiny. It is particularly important for healing to take place before entering new relationships. If this is not addressed, you will find yourself going back in the same circle, going back around again. Stop the cycle from occurring now. It is time to get off the merry-go-round. Keep in mind that the Lord is near the broken hearted. He can be a big help in forgiveness and healing if you let Him be a help for you.

> The Lord is near to those who have a broken heart, And saves such as have a contrite spirit. (Psalm 34:18)

This point is important to remember. Often the godly men are constantly telling their wives, "I did not do that to you." They get the consequences from the pain the bad boy caused. The godly men are accused of doing things that they have not done. It's a clear sign that the woman has not healed from the previous relationships. The pain that she has can be so deep that women turn away from the blessings that God is sending her way. It can be mentors, divine connections, even good healthy relationships, good desires of her heart.

Let's investigate this further. How can someone be deceived and continue to be in a relationship while everyone around them continues to warn the person? It has me to think about the decision that was placed before the people for someone to be crucified in biblical times: Barabbas or Jesus. The decision seemed to be a no brainer to pick Barabbas; however, they selected Jesus. Huh? Barabbas was a well-known criminal. which has been noted in Matthew 27:16. Peter spoke about Barabbas being a murderer in Acts 3:14. However, Jesus, who was without sin, was selected to be crucified. In reviewing more things about Barabbas, I see he participated in a rebellion against the government. Some called him a robber, terrorist, deceiver, and even an assassin. Don't be so judgmental about the group that chose to have Jesus crucified.

There was a lot of deception that took place that had a great influence on the people and their decision. An interesting thing about the two vastly different men is that their names have a similar meaning in the Hebrew language. There are two ironies about the name all according to Paul Sumner. One about the name Jesus being removed from Barabbas the terrorist. "Several manuscripts, however, name the terrorist "Jesus Barabbas" and quote Pilate as asking: "Whom do you want me to release for you, Jesus Barabbas or Jesus who is called the Messiah?" Many scholars believe the double name "Jesus Barabbas" was the original reading. They suggest that "Jesus" was omitted from Greek copies of Matthew out of reverence." "The second and deeper irony in the reading 'Jesus Barabbas' appears when we note that 'Barabbas' (or 'Bar Abbas') is the Hellenized form of the Aramaic name **Bar Abba**, meaning 'son of the father.' And the name 'Jesus' (Greek, Yesous) is the Hellenized form of the Hebrew name Yeshua," according to HebrewStreams.org article by Paul Sumner. One Jesus or the other Jesus.

Jesus said He was the Son of God. Many said this was blasphemy. You can even think about this being the culture of that day. They considered it to be blasphemy; however, not everyone felt the same way. Peter stated the same in the book of Matthew.

> Simon Peter answered and said, "You are the Christ, the Son of the living God."Jesus answered and said to him, "Blessed are you, Simon Bar-Jonah, for flesh and blood has not revealed this to you, but My Father who is in heaven." (Matthew 16:16-17)

As you can see, there were some that knew the truth and others that were deceived. Peter knew the truth about Jesus and denied Him three times. Deception is not the only thing that played a part. Pressure from other outside forces caused some to make the wrong decision. Unless you have a strong solid foundation, it can be hard to say what a person may do given the circumstances. God does not change regardless what occurs. What we would want to do is have the integrity to do the same: not to change regardless of the circumstances.

> Jesus Christ is the same yesterday, today, and forever. (Hebrews 13:8)

Even though Barabbas had a history of criminal activity, Jesus' actions were considered to be of a greater offense occurring to those that were there in attendance telling Pontius Pilate to crucify Jesus. If those that were in the audience would only look at the works from Jesus, the works have spoken and shown them that Jesus was the Son of God. Don't be deceived into picking the wrong man. I strongly encourage you to seek first the kingdom of God (Matthew 6:33). Seek the first man Christ Jesus. While seeking Him and putting Him first, He will guide you to finding the godly man.

At this point, some people may see themselves in the middle of what is mentioned. It may even bring back some memories that you would like to forget. I pray this provides some healing or this will be a help to someone else.

There are some things we can compare when looking at the bad boy and the godly man. You may be able to look at this and ask what I could have done differently? You can take this to consider what to think about with the next opportunity for a relationship. Not only a relationship with opposite sex regarding a mate, but other types of relationships such as business, community, friends, and other associations.

## GODLY MAN

- How much of himself has he given to God?
- He thinks long term
- He chooses to love (circumstances don't determine)
- He may seem boring
- Narrow is the way
- He works first and receives the rewards later

## BAD BOYS

- He loves until the next thing comes along
- He is exciting temporarily
- He does not commit
- He lives for the moment
- He may have a reference of God, but does not know God (no personal relationship)

## HOW MUCH OF HIMSELF HAS HE GIVEN TO GOD?

When looking at the man's life, how much of the life is devoted to God? Does the man have a relationship with God? Do you see the fruit of the Spirit operating in the man?

> But the fruit of the Spirit is love, joy, peace, longsuffering, kindness, goodness, faithfulness, gentleness, self-control. Against such there is no law. (Galatians 5:22-23)

Not to say the man is a Bible scholar, but it would be important to know when things get hard that he knows where to go and what to do. Does that relationship with God cause him to serve in the church? Again, not to say the person is an angel, but serving in the church can put the man around the right people.

> **He who walks with wise men will be wise, But the companion of fools will be destroyed. (Proverbs 13:20)**

It can also help strengthen current skills or develop new ones. His God-given talents and abilities can be discovered and begin to shine. He can do something that he has never done before in a supportive environment. When seeing these things, along with others, it can show the person's commitment to God and this can show how committed the person will be to you.

## HE THINKS LONG TERM

The godly man will think long term. He has the understanding that he will not be able to take someone out every night. Not that everything is perfect in his financial portfolio, if he has one, however the godly man would be taking steps to be a better steward in this area. The finances would only be one area. Decisions made today and how they would have an impact on tomorrow. Getting out of debt and clearing thing out. Being sure not to bring baggage along from unresolved issues in past relationships. Other parts of long-term thinking will be in ways that he can build for the future. This can include starting a business, going back to school, saving, or investing, depending on the personality. It can be some of these things or even more. Basically, a person that is thinking long term will keep working to develop themselves to prepare themselves for opportunities that would come in the future.

More importantly, he can think about how a future would be built with a future spouse. Questions can be asked about spending habits. It can feel like your entire lifestyle can be under a microscope. You may feel you are being interrogated at times. Don't be mad at the godly man when he is evaluating what it would take support a certain lifestyle or if changes would need to be made for the relationship to work long term.

> For which of you, intending to build a tower, does not sit down first and count the cost, whether he has enough to finish it... (Luke 14:28)

## HE CHOOSES TO LOVE.

A godly man understands that love is a choice and not a feeling. This does not mean that he has to tolerate anything, but he can choose to love you through everything. The love that he has for God will come through him to you. **The man will love his wife like Christ loves the church.**

This can be easier said than done. Regular church attendance, the right wife, family, and friends would all be a great team to help him to accomplish this type of love. The biggest and most important would be his relationship with God. However, this does not give you the right to continue to be a challenge to him, disrespect him, talk negatively about him, turn people against him, or make him look bad. Like I just said, you are to be part of the team, not his enemy. Things may not always go our way or be what we want. It would always be good to know that you have people that have your back. We know that God will have our back as we submit to Him. It is still good to see how He uses people in our lives that will do the same. Many can love you when things are going well, but when things change, the people change. There are others that say they need to teach you about love as if they are the expert.

The true expert not only teaches true love, but He also demonstrated it by His actions.

> **For God so loved the world that he gave his only begotten son that whosoever believes in him will not perish but would have everlasting life. (John 3:16)**

To know true love and how it works, we would need to look at what God has said in His Word. First Corinthians chapter 13 spells out what love is very plainly.

Even those that are doing things that are wrong will make it a practice to stick together. Things will be all bad all around them at times. They would have done wrong things that put them in this bad situation; however, they still manage to stick together and not back down. In some instances, they will fight for each other until the death because their commitment is so strong.

Something to think about: If they can do that being evil, are there many areas that we can improve in our relationships with one another? I would say **yes**. Instead of tearing one another down, we could work together and build. The synergy of at least two would more than double the power of one. One can put a thousand to flight and two can put ten thousand to flight (Deuteronomy 32:30).

## HE MAY SEEM BORING

If you have a life with a lot of excitement the godly man can seem boring to you at times. You may attend different parties with celebrity's day after day. Travel with exotic trips with yachts on vacations. Not to say that this will never happen again, however that godly man may go to locations as he is directed by God. The trips may be to places that are not exceedingly popular, however you can find safety because he is on assignment. Not the party that pops the Krystal over the 200,000-dollar cars, however you can see lives changed with some operating with a purpose.

## NARROW IS THE WAY

There is no need for this man to show off to try to impress. God will make him shine at the right time. **TRUST.** No one can do it better than God can. When all the exotic things fade, take a long hard look at what is around you at that point. Your real friends would be what you would most likely be able to find. They would be the ones that would have what I call the true unconditional love. When they can say, "Look, we don't have anything, but it is still all good."

Those are the friends that are there and don't need to show off to others to be accepted in any circle. They are true and confident in who they are and have solid foundation. They are not unsettled in anyway.

## HE WORKS FIRST AND RECEIVES THE REWARDS LATER

The godly man would be focused and limit his distractions. I'm sorry to say that not all his time will be spent on you. I don't mean to be negative in making this statement; however, I wanted to get you prepared for what may be coming down the road. As he is working and developing himself, he will learn how to manage his time with this new relationship that is on the horizon. It was mentioned earlier that he would be thinking long term and the activities that would involve.

Understand that everything will not be placed on hold for him to give you his undivided attention. Keep the bigger picture in mind. Something is being prepared for the future that this godly man would want you to be a part. This will help you long term, when you see him managing and balancing his time in the marriage in the future. He may not stop everything at once. Think about the future marriage for you. Appreciate the fact that he is learning to balance these things such as a marriage, children, career, and in-laws, just to name a few. I need to you understand that he will keep the job and work as unto the Lord on that job. With having more on his plate, with more responsibilities in all the different areas of his life, it can be a challenge. At this point in his life, relationships have developed in different areas such as church involvement, career, business, and other organizations. He will be more established and has gained the trust of those that he interacts. He will be working and developing more at the beginning. Get guidance from God, of course. He is working a process. Look for ways that you can team up together.

> And let us not grow weary while doing good, for in due season we shall reap if we do not lose heart. (Galatians 6:9)

The travels around the world will come later. The houses, cars, jewelry, and endless shopping trips can be at a later time. It would need to start from some point. Be patient. Understand the stage, or shall we say season, that you are in when you are currently in that stage/season. If his misses an item on your honey-do list, understand everything that he is juggling. Be patient. Look for ways that can make things easier for you both to work together. Keep the bigger picture in mind. Be patient.

> Though your beginning was small, Yet your latter end would increase abundantly. (Job 8:7)

## BAD BOY

### HE LOVES UNTIL THE NEXT THING COMES ALONG

A woman can have the bad boy's attention for a season, then suddenly, she can be changed for a totally different woman like a fashion trend. It can be easily seen how disloyal this person can be toward the woman. This is worse than what can be seen on the surface. This behavior can start as early as a school-age child. For example, the new girl comes to their school that everyone likes, and the bad boy drops his current girlfriend and gets with the new girl. All because he likes a challenge. This is a key here, to be careful what you attract. This bad boy likes a challenge at this young age.

What is he practicing at this young age? What is being developed in his character? Is this something that he may feel that he may need to do to keep up with others as peer pressure? Is this wired to his self-esteem to make him feel as if he is a man?

As this bad boy becomes an adult, we can see more of the same. Instead of it being the new girl in school, it is the new woman at the office, the apartment upstairs, or in the house across the street. As a young adult, the bad boy ways can still be part of their character if there has not been a change. People would ask, What ever happened to Donna? Well, Trina happened to Donna. Now that Trina is in the picture, Donna is an afterthought. Donna who?

Unfortunately, this can be brought into a marriage. I understand now why my pastor of so many years always discouraged dating for students. I have more respect for that now. I can see the damage it can do to both parties as they age. My father would always tell me over and over about different things, "When you are older, you will understand." Wow. The wisdom of waiting. Far too many times, we hear about the man leaving the home for different reasons.

It should not be a bigger challenge to encourage him to stay when the bad boy has his eye on another woman, but I am sure that it can be. The man has a family at stake here! This should not be a challenge to encourage him to stay, but it can be.

## HE IS EXCITING TEMPORARILY

When you see someone that is going out of his way to impress you, it can be flattering. Seeing him go over and beyond to make you think highly of him in all that he does and in all that he is doing in life. One thing that can be easily overlooked is that this is temporary. He can take you to the biggest parties with all the celebrities that you can name. He can have all the connections, claim to be working on different things, waiting on his ship to come in, but you don't see results. Don't get me wrong. Some things can take longer than others to get going. A new business can start slow and will take time to develop cliental. A real estate agent that just passed his exam would not start off being rich.

However, when you see a person wearing workout clothing all the time, you would expect to see some results at some point. If they continue to go to the gym, you would want to see some results. Unfortunately, after time, you find out it was all talk. You find that the nice car was not his car. The connections that he has helped him to get you to believe the lie that he may have been living.

By this time, you've gotten attached. No one could tell you anything before you got attached, but now you are attached. You have given him your heart because what you thought the relationship would become. Making excuses for him and for you to continue to be with him. Some may have given him more than just their heart at this point. Sexual relations may have taken place by now also, so you are really connected and attached. Don't get too caught up in the hype at this stage. There is a flip side.

## HE DOES NOT COMMIT

When thinking of a child in a candy store, they have a hard time making a choice. Understand that it can be a challenge to make a decision with so many types of candy and flavors to choose from. This can be a hard process for the bad boy. If he commits at any point, he will feel that he is missing out on everything else. He will want to have a long list of experiences before he settles. If he ever chooses to settle. Yes, the bad boy would be a player. This will be a bad thing because the feelings and emotions of all would be damaged. This will cause baggage to be brought to future relationships. If there are children involved, that could amplify the damaged that is caused.

King Solomon had 700 wives and 300 concubines (1 Kings 11:3). I am sure he had fun as a king being a bad boy with this many women at his beck and call. Sadly, they led him away from his destiny. When the time came for responsibility, I can only imagine how hard it would have been for him to spend time with the wives and children. There are only 365 days in a year. Not to say that Solomon was a bad man. He could easily be seen as an absentee father to his children if he had many by these different women. Some say he may have married some of the women to make allies with other kingdoms to prevent wars, even though there was not a war with his kingdom during the time as king. This could have been handled better.

An interesting thing to note is that in the book of Proverbs and the book of Ecclesiastes, there are verses about that one special woman.

## I WOULD ENCOURAGE YOU TO STRIVE TO BE THAT SPECIAL WOMAN

> May your fountain be blessed and may you rejoice in the wife of your youth. (Proverbs 5:18)

> Live joyfully with the wife whom you love all the days of your vain life which He has given you under the sun, all your days of vanity; for that is your portion in life, and in the labor which you perform under the sun. (Ecclesiastes 9:9)

Sounds like there is a lesson to learn about a man that is with one woman for a long time. Appears that Solomon still learned a lesson even though he had all the women the bad boy could dream of having.

This can be one relationship without all the baggage from all the others piling in and impacting the true God-given, God-ordained future where it would be easier for the destiny that the two will become one. More focus could be put on the marriage with less of the distractions outside of the marriage, such as other women, past girlfriends, baby mamas, past hurts, and drama coming from every direction. Even the wise man in the Bible learned something.

## HE LIVES FOR THE MOMENT

Just as mentioned in the section earlier, the bad boy would have fun. They only live for the moment. They do not think about the long-term consequences or how what they do would hurt others. They don't think about other aspects of the future. If it looks good and feels good. They will --- Just Do It!

This is when the bad boy wants to make a name for himself. It is not about others and the things he is doing to help others. The spotlight would be on him. How many women he has or how many he has had. (Not to put everything on the bad boy. There are women that do the same. Just to be clear.) Spotlight on how much money he is making, his popularity with everyone, and even the lifestyle that he is living.

Everything is about him and with him doing what he wants to do and how things please him. The bad boy wants to be the big shot at this point. He wants to show off to others as an attempt to impress or get respect from peers and those around them. The bad part is that it is at the expense of those that are close.

The girlfriend can be the grunt of the jokes. He goes into debt to buy things that he cannot afford to try to look bigger than he is to others. This is really bad because the name and reputation would be more important to him than the things that really matter. This cannot be above taking care of his children, education, different relationships with friends, family, and business. Most important is that this cannot come before his relationship with God. God provides a warning of this type of behavior in His Word.

> **For men will be lovers of themselves, lovers of money, boasters, proud, blasphemers, disobedient to parents, unthankful, unholy, unloving, unforgiving, slanderers, without self-control, brutal, despisers of good, traitors, headstrong, haughty, lovers of pleasure rather than lovers of God... Timothy 3:2-4**

Outsiders can use this to their advantage. If the bad boy wants to be a big shot, the financial predators can all get in line to get their piece of the action. They can get their piece of the pie. It is so subtle. It would be people that you would not have in mind. It can be bankers, jewelers, real estate agents, car salesmen, other women, friends, even strippers at the club.

He is not the only one that is aware when the bonus is coming. All the people in the group are aware and are calculating what they can get from his bonus. It can be from a deal that has been made, a property sold. Whatever the case. Outsiders can have plans for the bad boy's money, and if he is caught up in living for the moment, they will take it from him with no regard. They are able to do so because of his mindset and lifestyle.

## HE MAY HAVE A REFERENCE OF GOD, BUT DOES NOT KNOW GOD (NO PERSONAL RELATIONSHIP)

Many can attend church services on a regular basis. Just because the person is attending church services on the regular does not mean that they are what they pretend. Even if you find that the person is not what they seem, it would not be your place to change the person. This is an area that one would need to be careful. This is where a red flag would go up. If you are making excuses for the person and making every effort to be with them still, this is a problem.

There are only a few answers to the question as to why a person would be doing this at this point. The woman may be desperate. The woman has had sex with this person. What is worse is that this woman has given her heart to the man at this point. It is dangerous for a person to be in this state.

When talking about the bad boy living for the moment, God's Word talks about how men would be lovers of themselves. There is a warning that is provided in the latter part of the same chapter that address the dangers of a man that has a reference of God, but does not have a one-on-one relationship with God. He will not act on the power that comes with having a true relationship God. It is even stated to turn away from this type of person.

> ...having a form of godliness but denying its power. And from such people turn away! For of this sort are those who creep into households and make captives of gullible women loaded down with sins, led away by various lusts, always learning and never able to come to the knowledge of the truth. (2 Timothy 3:5-7)

It is important to take heed to the warning to turn away. This can be spotted earlier in the process following what Jesus said. Inspect the fruit.

> Even so, every good tree bears good fruit, but a bad tree bears bad fruit. A good tree cannot bear bad fruit, nor can a bad tree bear good fruit. Every tree that does not bear good fruit is cut down and thrown into the fire. Therefore by their fruits you will know them. (Matthew 7:17-20)

If you look at the fruit of the person, you will be able to determine where the person is at an earlier point in the relationship, at whatever point the relationship has developed, whether friendship or acquaintance. The same process can work on other types of relationships that you encounter. Surround yourself with those that have a one-on-one relationship with God and are not denying His power.

## WRAP UP

In summary, I would like to encourage you to make the right choice. Pick the right "Son of a Rabbi." Pick the right Jesus and not the wrong Barabbas. Most importantly, do not be deceived as they were on that day. Pick the right Jesus to rule in your life first and foremost. Let that Jesus lead you to the godly man. Do not be deceived. Don't think so short term. Think more long term and it will help you to make better choices about where to spend your time. If it is with the godly man, that would be great. Maybe it is not with anyone just yet. That is okay. You can invest this time preparing yourself.

You can use this time to be become the queen for your king that is to come. The queen is royalty, so she will conduct herself in a certain way. If the queen of a kingdom would have to learn and prepare herself for her role in the kingdom that she will serve, a woman would have to do the same for the role that she will take in a marriage. You're already destined to be the queen. There is nothing wrong with adding more value to yourself.

It is amazing how we can make all the efforts in the natural for things such as careers, projects, and education. Things are lacking when thinking about building families, building futures, or leaving a legacy. When you spend time with the bad boy, it will impact how you view the godly man. The bad boy will entice you with the exciting things and make you think he has more to offer than the godly man. As you spend time with the bad boy, the things that the godly man are about will tend to fade away. In the same fashion that the wrong women led the wise King Solomon out of his destiny, the bad boy will lead you out of destiny that God has for you.

There is a flip side that is not thought about up front. Do not be deceived. Don't find yourself in a place where you're being hit, have an STD, credit ran into the ground with everything that you worked for brought to nothing. Someone may even be doing jail time because of the bad boy. Not only staying with him because you have given your heart to him, but also finding yourself in survival mode and compromising where you know you don't need to compromise. Feeling that you need him in order to survive.

If you are in a situation and want the bad boy to change, you can believe God for him to change. Get yourself out of harm's way first and foremost, of course. **Forgive.** Read what I tell you next very carefully. **LET GOD CHANGE THE BAD BOY. <u>NOT YOU</u>. STAY OUT OF GOD'S WAY AND LET GOD BE GOD.** He will do a better job than you. God is smarter than us. God will do a better job. God knows him better than you. God will do a better job. **LET GOD CHANGE THE BAD BOY.** This will allow God to get the credit. <u>**NOT YOU**</u>. God does not need your wrong type of help. No need to drop hints. No need for mind games. No need to try to apply pressure from others. It is not about you impressing your friends. When you think you know what you are doing, you end up pushing him away and you are unaware. Again! **LET GOD CHANGE THE BAD BOY. <u>NOT</u> <u>YOU</u>. STAY OUT OF GOD'S WAY AND LET GOD BE GOD.** Just said that to be clear. You can pray for him and ask for God to change the person. Stay consistent in believing and do not speak against what you prayed for and believe. We call that <u>faith</u>. When we give God the credit, it makes such a greater impact.

As mentioned earlier, there are some things in the book that may be challenging to you when reading. Some may be offensive. Some you may not want to hear about. I tried to prep you by giving you a heads up. If you need to take a pause before going to the next chapter, it is understandable. You may need to reflect on some things. You may need to just calm down. Many things can affect the readers in different ways. When you are ready to go to the next chapter, strap in and let's take this ride.

# 2
# HE WON'T OPEN UP TO ME

Relationships can be going well, and then all of a sudden, things are not be what they used to be. People are not as close as they once were. I would not say that those in the relationship are drifting apart, but they are not as talkative as they once were. Finding out information that they were not told before. When the news came in, it was like you were the first to know. Now, you are the last to find out. Not only are you the last to find out, but you heard it from a third party or by accident.

There can be several reasons this occurs. During the relationship, over time, some may have learned that you have to limit the information that you share depending on the person, the personality, and things of that nature. This chapter can spell out some of the reasons that he may not be open to telling you everything about anything.

## YOU MAY NOT BE ABLE TO HANDLE THE TRUTH

If you made it to this chapter from the beginning of the letter, this may not apply to you. Again—it *may* not apply to you. If you turned to this chapter first, that is a good sign that this *does* apply to you.

When the truth is told, it can hurt. That is understandable; however, when that hurt is turned back on someone, that is not good. As the saying goes, "Don't kill the messenger."

When you lash out at the person that is telling you the truth, it does not encourage them to come back and tell you anything else in the future. If the building is on fire, someone is telling you the truth because they love you enough to tell you to allow you to prepare yourself to escape. You push them away when you lash out at them for trying to help you. That will cause the person to look out for themselves. They will get up and get out of the fire, hoping you got the clue. Then, at the end of day, you will ask, "Why did they not tell me?" Duh… You might be that person that it is hard for everyone to talk to about anything.

The truth can be like a huge statue in a living room. As some would say, there is an elephant in the room. No matter what is done, the statue would still be in place. We can yell at it. We can try to cover it up. We can try to camouflage it. We can try to decorate it. The statue would still be there. The truth can be the same way. You can try to do different things regarding the truth. It will still be there staring you right in the face.

On a positive note, some can look at feedback as a gift. It is a gift that you can use to develop yourself into becoming better at who you are or what you are doing. It can be in relationships, people skills, work, writing, cooking, or whatever it may be that you are involved. Honest feedback will be something that you can build upon. The truth may hurt, but God's Word says the truth will make you free.

> **And you shall know the truth, and the truth shall make you free. (John 8:32)**

I would encourage you to be more open to getting truth. Make any adjustments as needed. Become more teachable and more understanding. This can help you to move forward in a more positive light. People can feel more comfortable about giving you feedback at the point in your life that you would need it the most. You would not want to go the dream job interview with a stain on your shirt. A true friend would let you know before you walked into the office for the interview.

## YOU REPEAT EVERYTHING YOU HEAR

I cannot beat around the bush with this in any way. You talk too much. I love you too much not to tell you. I must be very direct with some things. I hate it when it is said, but the saying goes, "Telegraph, television, telephone, tell a woman. You just told everybody." This is not a good perception. If you are the type of person that would cut off a person when they answer a question that you asked them, this can be dangerous. What this means is that you would speak before you think about how your words would impact others. This is not the type of person that anyone would need to share information with.

Not only is the information repeated, it is often misinterpreted, misunderstood, exaggerated, and turned into an outright lie, causing people to jump to conclusions. When anyone is aware ahead of time that things would turn out in a negative fashion, they would not bother getting anything started. No one wants to spend so much time explaining everything, trying to clean up a mess that someone else created. This would be what is known as a talebearer.

> A talebearer reveals secrets, but he who is of a faithful spirit conceals a matter. (Proverbs 11:13)

Do not be offended by this section. Work on being the person that is of a faithful spirit. Be the person that he can count on that would have his best interest in mind, not the one that tells everyone about how he is wrong and then act as if he cannot function without you. Do not expect many heart-to-heart conversations if you repeat everything to everyone. As the older generations would say, "Don't put your business in the streets."

The things that the man would share with you would not need to be the neighborhood soap opera or drama. That would also be the same for the workspace, church, barbershop, hair salon, etc. Repeating everything would be a dishonor to him in so many ways. Just because you are upset with him does <u>not</u> excuse you from honoring the man. If you are of a faithful spirit, you would still conceal the matter. Even if you are mad at him. Situations like this would show true character.

A godly man will have different challenges to face in the world. A godly man would need to apply his faith in every situation. A godly man will have to fight what is known as the good fight of faith. The world can be against him. The devil is against him. His own fleshly desires are against him. People can be working against him to try to prevent him from getting ahead. That is enough for one person to bear alone. Do not add to the burden by informing the wrong people. That can add more problems. More people can speak against him and what he is doing. It can cause more people to work against his plans. You don't cast your pearls before swine.

> **Do not give what is holy to the dogs; nor cast your pearls before swine, lest they trample them under their feet, and turn and tear you in pieces. (Matthew 7:6)**

God's Word talks about what happens when you put what is valuable before the wrong people. People are not always who and what you think. I will emphasize that the wrong people can work against you and the godly man. As you can see in the Scripture, they can tear down what you and the godly man have worked to build. You might not get this part right away. Take a moment to think on what this is about and what this principle means. It may come to you over time. My dad would not always explain everything to me. Some things my dad would just say, "When you get older, you will understand." I have an understanding of those things now. In turn, I want to say to you, if you do not understand what I am talking about, come back to this section. I pray that you would ask God to give you the understanding.

Do not get in the habit of venting your feelings to others. This constant venting will breed gossip. Think about a group of people talking about you, saying negative things about you. How would that make you feel? Would this be a group of people that you would want to associate with by being around them? Probably not. When the negative things are spoken about the person that you are in a relationship with, they will not want to associate themselves with you or the group of people that you are venting to. The same group of people will turn right around and gossip about you both and the situation. This may seem harmless, but it is not. You can sit there and think he will just have to get over it and move forward. On the contrary, it does not work that way. The man will always want to be treated with honor. Things like this are dishonoring the man. Family functions, social gatherings, and other events will come up and he will not care to attend them with you, the reason being is that he does not know what you vented to them or why they are gossiping. He would probably just rather not be bothered. What I really hate is when he is asked to go to church and he does not care to come, being the same process is taking place in the church. At times with the same people. You've got to get a handle on this taking place. We need to stop things like this from being a roadblock for the men coming to church. It is like a person that has not been to church in a long time. When they come back once, they feel so judged that they decide not to come back again.

> A brother offended is harder to win than a strong city, and contentions are like the bars of a castle. (Proverbs 18:19)

> Whoever hides hatred has lying lips, and whoever spreads slander is a fool. (Proverbs 10:18)

Just because you are mad at the man does <u>not</u> give you a pass to be able to vent and put pearls before swine. You see what the swine will do to what you put in their presence. That was mentioned earlier in Matthew 7:6. Please do not learn this the hard way. **Stop venting.**

The perception is that venting is healthy. It is not. The trick is for the devil to get you in negative emotions to say and do wrong things, to continue to say the wrong things over and over, which would be the wrong confessions that you are putting out and not realize that you helping to cause these things to come to pass.

> Death and life are in the power of the tongue, and those who love it will eat its fruit. (Proverbs 18:21)

You vent and tell too much information about someone with whom you are in a relationship. The wrong person, or shall we say the swine, would feed on the information and use it to their advantage. This can be a person directly or someone standing by that is overhearing your conversation. The next week, you find yourself out of a relationship and see that you had a relationship with the wrong person, or shall we say the swine, accompanying them at the next event that you were planning to attend with the same person with whom you had the former relationship. You would not want to expose everything bad to the person that is trying to take your spot. That would not be wise. Venting is not a wise thing to do. If you do not believe me, take it from God's Word.

> A fool vents all his feelings, but a wise man holds them back. (Proverbs 29:11)

The godly woman, or shall we say the helpmate for the godly man, can stand beside him encouraging him, praying for him, limiting distractions from him, making a peaceful environment for him. She would consider him, so she would not leave him or his vision outside of her plans. She can be his mouthpiece. She can be his representation in his stead if he is not in place for whatever reason. The two can become one. Same mind, same judgment. Operate in sync with one another even if they are not at the same place physically. If you are a twin or grew up around a set of twins, this might be the closest example outside of a marriage that I can think about at the moment. Businesses and franchises consistently work to attain this even across different counties. One twin can buy a shirt at one store and the other twin would be at another store and purchase the same shirt without communicating. The two would find out they have the same thing when they got home. If you have Christ and the Holy Spirit, things like this can happen when you are both in tune with the Holy Spirit. The helpmate would be able to team up together with the godly man and this will allow them to accomplish so much more—TOGETHER.

In the Bible, there was a point that God told the children of Israel to walk around the wall of Jericho for six days without saying a word. Can you image not saying a word while walking around a large wall for six days without saying anything? On the seventh day, they were to give a big shout, then the miracle would take place for the wall to come down. It may take a miracle for some people to remain silent for six minutes, let alone marching around a wall silent for six days and shouting on the seventh. You may find it surprising that when you master that art of knowing when to be silent and when to speak and how to speak, you can have the miracle of them sharing more with you.

> **Even fools are thought wise if they keep silent, and discerning if they hold their tongues. (Proverbs 17:28)**

As the saying goes, if you keep silent, no one will know you are a fool until you open your mouth and prove to be otherwise. It can be a challenge to have a balance between being silent and speaking up. When you can become better at mastering the two, the man may open up more to you. The trust in this matter would have to be built. Just as if there is an abusive or cheating husband, he would have to build trust for others to believe in him. You would need to build trust again before he would believe that you have changed. This can get to the point where someone is thinking or even saying, "Do not keep telling me that you are changing. *Show* me that you are changing." This can take time to build this trust into your relationship. This may sound small, but it is a big thing to him. This would be part of honoring the godly man.

## IT MAY NOT BE THE TIME FOR YOU TO KNOW

Are you a person that is quick to react? Are you a person that is quick to jump to conclusions? People will have to take precautions before sharing information with you. They do not know how you will react. You may not hear the person out completely to get the full picture. It may not be the time for you to know. Your reaction may do more harm than good. You might do or say something to hurt someone. Tit for tat. You do not even have all the information. You cannot go back when damage is done. If you have a history of flying off the handle with a small bit of information, people will not be quick to tell.

Are you a person that wants to go all out? This can be good at times, but not all the time. When there is a budget to stay in and resources that you need to consider, you cannot go too far too fast. Things may be in place and going well, but everyone may need to hold off on telling you at the present time. The reason why would be because things will be done and promises made that involve others and causes money to be spent that they do not have at the moment. This brings unnecessary stress. It brings confusion and puts a burden on others and it should not bring this added weight. Wearing people thin. Wearing the budget thin. Wearing your resources thin. This really needs to be managed properly. When there is a tragedy and all these things are needed, you have little to nothing to fall back on to help. It can be an opportunity that comes that you could have taken advantage of, but now you cannot because you do not have what is needed to move forward.

This is like someone living in a small town in the south. There is not a lot of snow that comes in the south outside of the mountains. When there is a forecast of inclement weather, trucks run and de-ice all the roads. Milk and bread will be purchased in the stores. When the day comes for the inclement weather, nothing happens. Everyone is glad, but the real storm comes up the next week and all the resources are depleted. Food has been purchased from the stores. The workers that would drive the trucks or those that would make the other preparations are worn out. They are already tired from all that they did the week before. The storm comes and people are not prepared. Not mentally. Not physically. They are only tired. Many mistakes can occur when a person is in this state.

In the same regard as this example, you do not want to overdo things. It will not be just you speaking for yourself in every situation. Consider the weight that it may put on others. If you are on a committee for an organization, do not volunteer your family, friends, husband, or boyfriend to do things that you have not discussed with them first. Do not assume or say you're not doing anything else. They will not tell you about their calendar or plans any time soon. You can volunteer everyone to make yourself look good to the committee at the meeting and then put all the work on everyone else. Discuss things with everyone before you bring them up in a meeting. This will help everyone. Stop volunteering people and getting mad at them when they have to tell you no. Do not assume.

Something else to watch out for is to not push for things you are not ready or seasoned to handle at the present time. Like standing at the very top of a ladder and trying to stretch for something that is beyond your reach. The best practice is not to go higher than the top three steps and you are standing at the top! This is extremely dangerous. You have set yourself up for a great fall. The same thing occurs when you try to overextend yourself. This is also an extremely dangerous state. Do not be tempted and fall into this trap. This is how people get into debt. This is how people make big promises that they cannot deliver. They overwork themselves and get sick. Do not try to impress people. As I was told, "Impress God." Let God impress the people. Do not fall into that trap. Keep your sanity. Live, work, and play within your means.

It may not be you at all. It could be the people that you are surrounded by. Be careful regarding the company that you keep. Realize the company that you keep and the influence that they have over you. Will they be careful with what they are exposed? You may be a person that does not repeat anything, but the people that you hang around tell everything. A bad influence will have different negative effects on you. It may not be the right time to tell you because the company that you have may not manage the information that is given to you properly.

> Do not be deceived: "Evil company corrupts good habits." 1 (Corinthians 15:33)

Consistently take an evaluation of those that you keep company with. Birds of a feather flock together. Do not get labeled with the wrong label.

## YOU MAY BE TOO CONTROLLING

If you are a controlling person or have a controlling type of personality, this may be another reason why he is not opening up to you. This type of person would take things over. Everything will have to go the way that they think they should go. If others will not do what they want them to do, they will have a price to pay. This type of bully trait can be seen across different relationships: family, work, volunteer organizations, neighbors, etc.

When the controlling person takes over, that person can make bad decisions. There can be good counsel all around them and they will still make a bad decision. This is something that we will go into more detail bout this later in this chapter. This controlling person can often remove things from people that were destined to do them to bless others. That can place a stumbling block in front of them, preventing them from enhancing the gift that God gave. There are times that you will need to give family, friends, and others room to make mistakes. They will be able to grow develop and learn from their mistakes.

> From whom the whole body, joined and knit together by what every joint supplies, according to the effective working by which every part does its share, causes growth of the body for the edifying of itself in love. (Ephesians 4:16)

As the saying goes, "If mama ain't happy, ain't nobody happy." This sounds to me like this is a woman that runs her house through manipulation. Everyone in the house operates out of fear instead of them all working together to add value. It all goes back to the control of having it her own way. Other suggestions do not matter. Do not be this person. If you are this person, I would encourage you to work on making a change.

> For rebellion is as the sin of witchcraft, and stubbornness is as iniquity and idolatry. Because you have rejected the word of the Lord, He also has rejected you from being king. (1 Samuel 15:23)

It can be hard to open up to a person that is stubborn and controlling. You will find this person cutting people off while they are talking, dominating or controlling the conversation, and limiting the input that others try to place in the conversations, as if others' input is not of any importance.

Questions are asked like, "Who are you talking to?" "Why are you around them?" "Why is this being done this way?" It is often rooted in insecurity and self-centeredness. When someone operates in fear of someone having a better idea or losing them to someone else, all the questions come up. To avoid conflict, others will just not say anything or get any input from anyone other than you. Comments would be made, such as, "You know how she is." "That is the reason why I asked you instead." "She is difficult to talk to." Do not let actions like this stop progress that could be made.

Work with those that are around you and consider their input.

You may be surprised. You may learn a thing or two. When every joint will supply, as the Bible verse mentions, the different giftings can come together and add more value. The outcome can be greater than you ever expected for it to become.

## NEGATIVE AND NOT SUPPORTIVE OF DREAMS

Do you always have something negative to say about his dreams, hopes, and desires? No one wants to share their dreams with dream killers. You will have to take a good look here, because if this is you, you may be part of the swine that was mentioned earlier. This man had hopes and dreams before he ever met you. If he is ever at a point that he is making a sacrifice, do not put them down. People with dreams may have to invest their time, money, resources, and talent for their dream, understanding that there is a limit. This cannot take away from responsibilities. Those cannot be neglected; however, there can be several cutbacks.

You may not be going out as much. You may not get as much of undivided attention as you did in the past. Not shopping as much. Not spending as much time with friends. This can be a time that some of the big decisions would be made. Would activities need to be cut out? Would he need to evaluate the friend? As we discussed before about the swine, who could he share these things with and talk about his progress? If you are saying it should be you, I would agree. It *should* be you. Look at the criteria in this chapter and ask yourself if you qualify. I hope you are not the swine in this scenario. We all have room to improve. I would encourage you to make yourself more of a person that someone would want to share their hopes and dreams. Someone that can be trusted. This can give God something to work with in having you work together. Iron can sharpen iron.

> As iron sharpens iron, so a man sharpens the countenance of his friend. (Proverbs 27:17)

By the iron sharpening iron, everyone can grow and accomplish more. When the man has tunnel vision for the goal that he is striving for, it would be all that he talks about and may seem that is all that he has time for on his calendar. Be the help and not a hinderance. This phase can be critical, so he can put all his focus on this vision or plan. Even Jesus said that if you are not with Him, you are against Him.

**He who is not with Me is against Me, and he who does not gather with Me scatters abroad. (Matthew 12:30)**

Do not take this the wrong way. Positive support is needed at this time. Distractions would need to be eliminated. Things that are being done at this time would need to add value. Do not look at what he is doing as something small that can be overlooked. It is important to him and could be leading him to the destiny that God has for him. If that is the case, wouldn't it be great to go down in history as the someone that took part in making the vision come to pass instead of the person that killed the dream?

The vision is not valued by the amount of money that it brings home. If that is all you are thinking about, you are shallow. If his vision is something that God is in, I can assure you that it will help others. When God has someone do something, He will provide for them and take care of the person or group of people. Stop putting pressure on the man when he is doing what he needs to do, when he is doing what he can do with the vision or dream and taking care of the other responsibilities. This is not the time to be pushing for extras. Look to God. Your day is coming. You will get a return for all you have done. Keep your eyes on God and not the man. I'm encouraging you to make God your source. He's got you!

Someone is reading this and saying, "That is all well and good, but the man I am with does not have a vision. He does not work toward anything." First, make sure you are a person that he can share a vision with and have a discussion. Once you have determined that you have met that condition, you can look for ways to expose him to more.

Enlarge the vision for you both. Look at bigger things yourself. Let him see you looking into opportunities to better yourself and go to another level. If he asks you questions like, "What you doing?" you can show him. Not nag him. Show him. Put him and yourself around people that are working on going up to the next level. Like I said before, he can work some projects with people that have made some achievements in their lives and that can motivate him to have a vision. There is the internet, you can go for a walk, take a drive, look at the positive things on TV, or even read the Bible together. There are many people and stories in the Bible that can spark an interest. You do not have to spend a lot of money to be inspired. The vision will have a cost. It will be worth the price.

Someone else is reading this and saying, "I do not have a man." You can enlarge your vision just like the person that has a man that does not have a vision. You will never go higher than where your vision places you. See yourself with someone. What kind of person will you be for the person that you have in this vision? Now work on being the person that God would have for them as a partner, friend, spouse, etc. Be that woman that someone could not live without having in their life. A woman of character, trust, integrity, work ethic, and loyalty. Not looking to take, but looking to add value. Do not be insecure and do different things like plastic surgery and starving yourself out of fear of not being with someone. Be healthy for the right reasons. When you look at things long term, the character traits can outweigh the temporary things that are done out of fear. Work on the right things that will last a lifetime. Be the woman that he would want to have in his corner.

## COMPETITION

You cannot have a relationship to compete with each other. What you should do is complement one another. You can live with the persona that you continue to try to outdo one another. You have nothing to prove. If you are in a relationship with the person, you have already proven yourself. He will hold off on bringing things to your attention when you have to turn everything into a competition, always making a show before an audience that you can always do things better. This is not being supportive.

> How could one chase a thousand, and two put ten thousand to flight, Unless their Rock had sold them, And the Lord had surrendered them? (Deuteronomy 32:30)

As mentioned before, there is so much more that can be achieved by you working together. You are not going to get ahead working against each other. Jesus even warned that a city or a house divided against itself cannot stand. What a strong force that can be made as when the two are working side by side.

> But Jesus knew their thoughts, and said to them: "Every kingdom divided against itself is brought to desolation, and every city or house divided against itself will not stand." (Matthew 12:25)

Do not put on the show to be the center or have the spotlight on yourself. You have a special person in your life. Value that relationship by valuing the person. The price of getting the spotlight and amusing the audience is not worth the outcome. Especially if the audience in only gossiping behind your back anyway. When others look at you do this, they will turn around and do the same thing. In the end, it seems that everyone is having problems in their relationships. Do not be the fool. As I said earlier in this chapter, do not try to impress people. Try to impress God. Always look to do things God's way. His reward will be far greater than what any audience will do for you with the show that you perform. Again, you have nothing to prove.

## YOU JUST DON'T LISTEN

As mentioned in the "you may too controlling" section earlier, the fact that you are not listening can be an important factor to consider as to why he is not opening up to you. Others with expertise, giftings, and talent could be telling you what you need to know, but you still do not listen. You still will not listen to good sound judgment. If there are matters that you cannot disclose and information that you need to keep confidential, that is understandable, but when you just dismiss everything everyone has to say, that is a problem. You must listen to somebody. God's Word mentions it is good to get help from the right people.

> For by wise counsel you will wage your own war, and in a multitude of counselors there is safety. (Proverbs 24:6)

When you have the right people in your corner, you get things accomplished. It is up to you to receive them in your situation. You may not have everyone and everything you want the entire time, however God will never leave you or forsake you. You will always have God.

Some make winning the argument and being right more important than doing what is right. I would often tell the children that I work with that God gave you two eyes, two ears, and one month. You need to pay attention and listen twice as much as you are speaking. We will all want to do this and not react out of our emotions.

> So then, my beloved brethren, let every man be swift to hear, slow to speak, slow to wrath... (James 1:19)

It would be more important to maintain the relationships with the people than being right or winning the argument. It is not healthy in relationships to be so quick to ask or answer questions to cut others off so only your point can be heard. Let us be careful that we are not in pride because pride goes before destruction.

> Pride goes before destruction, And a haughty spirit before a fall. (Proverbs 16:18)

Talk to the person out of love. Give them your undivided attention. Show them that what they have to say is important. Do not let them feel as if they are under attack. Hear them out completely. Again, hear them out completely. They will be more comfortable to talk to you more.

## WRAP UP

If you feel distant from him and cannot seem to reconnect, think about the topics in this chapter. At the end of each chapter is a time of reflection. There will be not be any finger pointing. Only reflection of self. What is it that you have the power within yourself to change? No one has to know. As far as anyone can see, you are reading a book. Any personal adjustments can remain private. I would suggest praying and allowing God to show some things to you. It is quite easy for us to highlight what we want to address and leave everything else the same. That only causes us to have the same issues that we had earlier.

This is not to make a change to get something quick in return. If there is a change that needs to be made, have the heart to make the change regardless if he wants to connect back with you or not. The results in the relationship connection may not be quick. In the microwave society, things may now happen as fast we would like; however, over time, you may see a better connection take place. The reason the better connection can take place is because the change would be made in your heart. When the change is made in your heart, it would please God because you would have the right motive. People will see the change from your actions and from how you speak. Out of the abundance of the heart the mouth will speak.

Look to receive information without getting into your emotions. Block the negative emotions from hindering you from moving forward. Keep things private and confidential. If you use the things that he tells you against him, you will shut the door on him sharing things with you in the future. Release the control in the areas that you need to let go of the reins. Hear things out and get the full picture. Look for ways to encourage and work together.

If you have come to this point in the letter, you are starting the see how things are laid out and how they are being addressed. That is, if you have read from the beginning of this book. This is all from a heart that wants you to be successful in all your relationships—not just at home, but with every person or relationship that you encounter. This ride can have ups and downs. Stay strapped in and let's go to the next chapter.

# 3

# COMMUNICATION

There was a friend of the family that dated a lady at his job. He worked in a corporate environment. There was a large number of people that worked on the same floor with him and the lady that he was dating. Can you image the challenges that could take place with having a relationship in the workplace with over hundred people working on the same floor? Not to mention, the building or the entire company. The main example that comes to mind is how he said people would come to him and make comments about what he was doing during the upcoming weekend. It would be his first time that he heard about the plans. I know that must have been frustrating for him to get the updates from everyone but the lady that he was dating. They all knew his weekend plans before he ever found out. It finally got to the point that he told her that this is not going to work. He no longer dated this lady.

There are many dynamics with the example that could be brought out. Different things that can be discussed in this one small example; however, this chapter is about communication. The main thing that could be seen in the example is that the lady did not communicate to the man. The young lady had her different activities in mind. I am sure that she had great ideas. She never took the time to talk to the person that she was making plans to spend the time with during these activities. It is like he did not have an opinion or any voice on what was to be done. The is one of the big items that is often thought about when we think about communication issues. There is so much more that is involved.

There can also be confusion, being that words have different meanings. There are other barriers with the language that can prevent everyone from communicating the way they would like. You can take two people that grew up in the same region of the same county that speak the same language and they can still have issues communicating. Communication is a two-way street. There is a giving side where the message is being sent and a receiving side where the message is being received. Let's look at the some of the dynamics.

There is a theory by Professor Albert Mehrabian of University of California, Los Angeles, that there is a breakdown for communications. The breakdown would come to 7% words, 38% voice quality, and 55% non-verbal cues. We all do not realize that what is coming out of our mouths is only 7% of the message that is being received. When there is a conflict that people are trying to work out or settle, the comment is always made, "They didn't have to say it that way." When a person is in their emotions, they are not thinking about all these things. The person is only human, right?

We need to watch what is being said and how it is being said. When the wrong comments are made, or the wrong message is sent, it is not like you can always take them back. The words can hurt, and they can cut. The wounded person can find it hard to receive comfort from the same mouth that just finished cutting them in their heart. A person must be careful with the presentation and the delivery of the message. Especially with children. We all need to make the extra effort on crafting the messages sent to them and how they are treated when we deliver the message to them. What are some other things that we would need consider when communicating?

## HOW IMPORTANT IS IT TO YOU?

I think about Fortune 500 companies and all the effort they put into communications. Looking at over 3 million dollars for a minute-long commercial during the Super Bowl. They make every effort to get the right message across the first time. They do not want to have any miscommunications. No misunderstanding. They are willing to put a lot of time and money behind the communications that they send. Immediately you can see how important communications are to the different companies. That would be across the board: entertainment, financial, medical, law practices, and manufacturing, just to name a few. They all continue to do things repeatedly to be sure that they have everything correct before moving forward.

If you can think about a singer in a recording studio with a recording producer and executives all waiting for the singer to hit the right note vocally. The recording producer and the executives from the record company can seem picky or act as if they are just perfectionists. The reason that they have everything under a microscope is because they are seeking a return on everything that is invested in the project that they are working on with the singer. They have a lot on the line. Their job could even be on the line.

Careful thought is put into the information. What is the point to get across? How will it be presented? A budget is placed around everything that will be done. Different projects would consist of different needs. There could be a need for graphics, actors, music, technology, and other things of this nature. Surveys can be taken to see how the audience will receive the communication. This will help them to see if everything that they are doing will hit the target that they trying to reach.

Even after 9/11, with the fears that took place with flying at that time, corporations started to fly again. The corporations would send their employees across the nation and even across the world to other countries. These corporations feel it is important for the meeting to take place face to face. Just hearing someone's voice over a conference call was not enough. They want and need to get the entire message from those with whom they are conducting business. The same takes place with projects and products and services being developed. They will try to get as close to face-to-face meetings as possible. The companies understand the need to be able to read the body language, hand gestures, and facial expressions. They look to see if the person makes eye contact or if the person has something to hide. The corporations invest to get this information. They understand the importance of getting the details.

What are you willing to invest into your relationship? What are you willing to invest in your communication? How important is it to you? It was mentioned earlier how the communication that you send is not just with your words. You need to consider the "how." How are you sending your communication to him, or to others? Just as you would read everything about a man when he is speaking to you, you need to think about all the signals when you are sending in a message to him. Are your arms crossed with your head twitching? Are your eyes rolling? Are you turning away and putting your back toward the person? Are you sucking on your teeth or making loud sighs? Are you yelling to talk over the other person? Are you cutting the person off when they are trying to speak? The actions taken along with the body language will impact what you are saying. They often take away from your message. Your audience can remember the actions more than what was said.

The negative things seem to stay in someone's memory more than the positive things said or done. Think about your childhood. How quick is it to remember the negative things done or said to you by others? Funny how those negative things come to mind so fast. It is like those things were imparted into us without us being aware. Unfortunately, some people do not care that what they are saying is going to impact the other person. They only care about getting their point across. When you put the words out there, you might be able to take them back. People can always say, "I take that back" when they see that they made a mistake. You might be able to take back the words, but you will never be able to take back the hurt. Think about it.

Now that we understand the different aspects of communication, we can look at taking a different approach. First and foremost, we would want to consider the tone that we take when speaking.

> A soft answer turns away wrath, but a harsh word stirs up anger. (Proverbs 15:1)

Again, you do not have to yell in order to be heard. If the other party continues to go on and on, be patient. There will come a time that you will be able to speak. They will come to a point that they will ask a question and wait for your response. If you are cut off while you are trying to respond, the person is terribly upset or only interested in getting their point across. They are not willing to listen and process what you are saying. You may want to wait for them to calm down or get in a better state that they can hear and reason better. The emotions can have a strong impact on a person's reasoning and their choices depending on how well they can manage their emotions.

When looking at the other items with the "how," think about the message coming from the right heart. Let others see that you have a heart that wants to work with them to resolve the issue or help everyone be successful.

> Hatred stirs up strife, but love covers all sins. (Proverbs 10:12)

> He who covers a transgression seeks love, but he who repeats a matter separates friends. (Proverbs 17:9)

Let us not add fuel to the fire or a burning building. Let us put the fire out. Treat the person the way you would want to be treated. Put the emotions and attitude aside. You would not like for someone to make the wrong gestures toward you when speaking to you, so give others the same respect. Listening will be just as important as speaking. Give others your undivided attention. This will help them to take you more seriously. You want to show them that you are opening a door for them to continue to communicate to you and not keep things from you. Let the communication be in love toward the person, regardless of the setting, whether it is with the spouse, children, co-workers, or volunteers. Make sure that it is sincere. If it is not, people will be able to see right through you, especially children. Just a word of caution. A child may call you out if you are saying something and you are not being sincere.

There is a biblical account where a cupbearer named Nehemiah was the servant to King Artaxerxes. The cupbearer is a high position that is held, as this person would be with the king and take care of the king's needs. Nehemiah was informed about the bad condition of the city where his ancestors were buried. Nehemiah did not have to say a word. The king saw the emotional state that Nehemiah was in by looking at his face.

> And it came to pass in the month of Nisan, in the twentieth year of King Artaxerxes, when wine was before him, that I took the wine and gave it to the king. Now I had never been sad in his presence before. Therefore the king said to me, "Why is your face sad, since you are not sick? This is nothing but sorrow of heart." So I became dreadfully afraid, and said to the king, "May the king live forever! Why should my face not be sad, when the city, the place of my fathers' tombs, lies waste, and its gates are burned with fire?"Then the king said to me, "What do you request?" (Nehemiah 2:1-4)

Nehemiah was afraid because it is not a good thing to show sadness in the king's presence. The king can have servants executed for showing sadness. During this time, those that were wearing mourning clothes would not be allowed into the palace, so for the king to single him out would have him think that the king speaking to him this way would have a bad outcome.

Notice that regardless of the situation Nehemiah was in, he was able to put his emotions aside and address what needed to be addressed. The city needed to be rebuilt. He prayed to God in chapter

1, and it can be seen how God is answering him with the favor from the king.

Just as Fortune 500 companies will prepare their communications for their audience, you can do the same. As you get to know others better, you can better prepare your message for your audience. As you get to know them better, you will be better equipped to prepare your communications. You will want to be sure that your message is understood the first time. Do not leave people wondering, "What did she mean by that?" Make sure your message is clear. Cover the topics and details that need to be covered. Eliminate any confusion.

## ASSUMPTION

One of the examples for this type of behavior would be when you are in conversation with someone and they consistently cut you off as if they knew what you were going to say. They did not take the time to hear was is actually being said. This can be dangerous in arguments when everyone is trying so hard to be heard and no one is listening. Some can think that doing this and finishing the sentences for someone will speed up the process to get to the point, but it does not. It will prolong the conversation, argument, or someone telling their side of the story. Do not feel singled out, because both men and women are guilty of doing this when communicating.

> A fool has no delight in understanding, But in expressing his own heart. (Proverbs 18:2)

> He who answers a matter before he hears it, It is folly and shame to him. Proverbs (18:13)

We all need to work on listening more.

Certain things develop in all of us at an early age that we do not even realize have taken place. These filters start at a point in our lives that can develop and become stronger as we get older if we do not renew our mind. You can look at these filters as mindsets: feelings toward a person, group of people, places, or things. An example of this can be when there is a meeting in the workplace. The youngest person can have an idea and they bring it up in the meeting. The group ignores the young person and an older person would bring up the same thing and get credit for the whole idea.

What has taken place here? The group has a filter, or shall we say mindset, that young people do not know anything, have no experience, and do not take anything seriously, so the group does not take the young person seriously. It is like they have profiled the person before they ever opened their mouth. I have been in this situation before. When I was in college, there was a meeting with other students to plan a show. Many of us were meeting for the first time. The question came up, "Where is everyone from?" Right after the question, a finger was pointed directly at me and the statement was made, "We know that he is from the south." Just like that, I was labeled. I had only said two words since I walked in the room. These two examples can show you the filters that have developed in the audience that are listening to what is being said. The filters can range from educated to non-educated, rich or poor, young and old, experienced and not experienced, man or woman, even saved or not saved. The filters can play a major factor in the communication. It was mentioned earlier in this chapter that there are two sides: one is sending the message and the other is receiving the message. The filters are more about the receiving side and how the message is being received.

Some of the disciples of Jesus had some challenges with filters/preconceptions that others had about them and their background. Many of the disciples were young. They did not all grow up in the synagogues or became a rabbi like the Pharisees or others.

> **Now when they saw the boldness of Peter and John, and perceived that they were uneducated and untrained men, they marveled. And they realized that they had been with Jesus. (Acts 4:13)**

Because they did not have the legacy or the background of others, they were not taken seriously; however, as we can see, that changed when not only did the people see the boldness, but the miracles. The proof was in the pudding. God backed them up.

Jesus had a challenge with the filters against Him. People did not realize that the person right in front of them could help them in their situation. Here are examples of two accounts.

> "Is this not the carpenter, the Son of Mary, and brother of James, Joses, Judas, and Simon? And are not His sisters here with us?" So they were offended at Him. But Jesus said to them, "A prophet is not without honor except in his own country, among his own relatives, and in his own house." Now He could do no mighty work there, except that He laid His hands on a few sick people and healed them. (Mark 6:3-5)

The people were limited on what they received from Jesus because of their filter toward Jesus. In this example, we can say their unbelief caused them to miss out on what God had planned for their lives. Our filters will need to be changed with a renewed mind. (Philippians 4:22-23).

> The queen of the South will rise up in the judgment with this generation and condemn it, for she came from the ends of the earth to hear the wisdom of Solomon; and indeed a greater than Solomon is here. (Matthew 12:42)

In the second account, Jesus is speaking about the men of Nineveh repenting at the preaching of Jonah and Queen of Sheba and kings coming from a long distance to hear King Solomon's wisdom. He was making a point that He was one that is greater than both Jonah and King Solomon. As you can see, the filters that were in the minds of the people prevented them from seeing Jesus as the Son of God.

You must be careful about what filters may be trying to form inside of you. They are so subtle, you will not even realize that they are even forming. The filter can form in the movies that you watch, media, news, social media, magazines, or people all around you. If you want to stay grounded, let the Bible be your anchor. Let the Bible settle every argument. Line up everything that you hear with what the Bible says. If it does not line up with God's Word, leave it alone. Stay with the truth.

There are those that will want you to think a certain way and make you do certain things. You can track it all back to how the different things are supported. Look at the films and television shows that are funded and take a deeper look at the message they are sending. The filters are planted in you to go against the things that God would want you to have in your life. I encourage you not to take the bait. Even if the movie is sooo good and the topic on social media is sooo great, we cannot let these things destroy our relationships, community, and families. It is bad that this type of brainwashing is taking place. What is worse is when they get you to pay for them to perform the brainwashing to all.

The way to remove the filters is by renewing your mind. The Word of God helps us with telling us what we need to do. This would be the anchor to help us to stay grounded: renew the mind.

> ...that you put off, concerning your former conduct, the old man which grows corrupt according to the deceitful lusts, and be renewed in the spirit of your mind. (Ephesians 4:22-23)

Another mistake that is often made as an assumption is to believe the other person knows and understands how you feel about everything. When you go on and on and tell all your problems to everyone, it is not good. I spoke about this in an earlier chapter. Not only are problems shared with the wrong person who can work against you, the wrong people would use the details to their advantage to go after what they want. They can try to pursue a relationship with the person you are in a relationship with or even try to pursue a relationship with you. That wrong person can seem to be so nice and understanding and you claim the person that you are in a relationship with is not as nice and understanding. The person you are with does not know how to be there for you. The problem is that all the conversations you had should have only been with the person you are in a relationship with. The time spent talking about all your problems to everyone else gave them the opportunity to know you better and they learned more about you. If that time and information had been spent with the person that you are in a relationship with, you would have received even better results.

The person that you are in a relationship with feels that you left them out of the loop. You cannot point the finger at them only. Take ownership for the part that you played. The man would have asked, "What is wrong?" or "Are you okay?" But you were in your "I am not speaking to you" mode, then vented to everyone else. This is not communication. Do not assume that he knows. You have to communicate to him. Do not assume. The person that you vented to knows you better now and can pursue to get whatever they want from you. After they have conquered what they want, they leave you hanging. What now? I would encourage you to consider these patterns. They are not healthy.

The man may not have grown up in the same environment that you grew up. He may not have grown up with the same influences in his life that you have in yours. He may not have been taught the same things that you have been taught. He may not have been exposed to the same things that you have. I'm not making excuses for him, but I am saying that the man may not have the same mindset as you. That does not mean the man is crazy because he does not agree with you. Two people with different mindsets can think differently. That is normal at the beginning. The Bible even states that married couples are to become one—meaning they did not arrive at being one on the first day of marriage.

> **For this reason a man shall leave his father and mother and be joined to his wife, and the two shall become one flesh. (Ephesians 5:31)**

Yes, they are married, but we all know that there would be some time for them to get adjusted. Do not assume that he will do everything the way you would. This would continue to be the part of you both getting to know one another.

## DIRECT COMMUNICATION

He needs to hear your heart, not the heart of those around you. If he has been around you long enough, he can tell that if what you are saying is from you and if what you are saying is coming from others. Think about parents talking to their small five-year-old. They can tell when different language, thoughts, or concepts are coming into their home. The parents will ask, "Where did you get that from?" "We did not teach this to you." "We don't talk that way." It is not the child's personality. The parents can tell that the child is being influenced by someone. In the same way, the man can tell how your thought process is being influenced by others.

It is what is coming from your heart that will matter the most, not what others are suggesting. You are the person that is in this relationship, not them. Do not think it strange, but people change and their options change. What they are telling you to do today could be something different tomorrow. Whatever you decide to do, make sure it lines up with the right thing to do. As an example, you might wake up on one cold winter morning, and you know in your heart you do not feel like getting up and out of that warm bed. The friends on the phone might tell you to stay home and not go to work. You get off the phone and communicate you do not feel like going, but you are getting up and going to work anyway. The husband may be glad to see you pressing through as he is getting up and ready to go to work. The good work ethic that you have may have been one of things that attracted him to you. Keep doing the right thing. Do not let the wrong influences invade your home or your relationships.

Direct communication is the best communication. The message is not distorted with others adding to the message or taking from the message. No matter what the content, you and the other person can come to an understanding quicker. This can cut down a lot of confusion. There is quicker conflict resolution when doing it this way. Social media, email, and text are all areas where you need to be careful. If you are sending negative things about someone, it is not just the person you are sending the negative things to for the moment. You are sending this negative information to the world. Someone can take your message and post it anywhere. Any time. You will not be able to take it back. Especially once the damage has been done. Face-to-face, one-on-one would be a better approach. Here are some Bible verses that advise this method.

> **Moreover if your brother sins against you, go and tell him his fault between you and him alone. If he hears you, you have gained your brother. But if he will not hear, take with you one or two more, that 'by the mouth of two or three witnesses every word may be established.' (Matthew 18:15-16)**

> Debate your case with your neighbor, And do not disclose the secret to another; Lest he who hears it expose your shame, And your reputation be ruined. (Proverbs 25:9-10)

I spoke with someone that was from a corporate background. He was in a different work environment working under a lady that was over his department. This environment was more laid back. Some of the staff would tell him to lose the suit. He was making sure things were done that needed to be done. I could tell because he could be aggressive at times. One day, the lady over the department that he was working for had him come and sit down because they needed to talk. Wow, what she expressed to him in that discussion. She was calm, but direct. She started off saying, "Hey, you are going to get your success that you have coming to you." She stated that she had people that should be calling for *her* calling in and asking for *him*. He was doing things that she should be doing. It was like she did not get her say earlier in the process. She made it clear to him that if she felt threatened, she would have to let him go. If she felt that he was taking her place, she would let him go.

I must say, regardless of how you feel about the situation or circumstance, there are a few things that I like about this conversation. There are a lot of bad things that anyone could point out, but I wanted to point out the good for the topic of this chapter. She spoke to him one on one. She did not single him out in front of a group. She did not talk about him to everyone in the office. She spoke to him directly. Next, I like is that she was honest: good, bad, or indifferent. She told the truth about how she felt and laid everything all out. She could have approached it differently, but she communicated everything she was feeling. This gives them something to work on. I am glad that she spelled it all out. Dropping hints is not going to get it. You must communicate. She ended the conversations just as she began: "You are going to get your success that you have coming to you."

Speaking one on one may cause you to get a more favorable response. The person is not put on the spot or singled out in front of a group. They may not be as defensive because they are only speaking with you. There are no outside influences or distractions. You can work together and have an honest talk to resolve in a healthier manner.

## COMMUNICATION WITH GOD

There is a message being sent (prayer) and a message to be received (are you listening?). Yes, God is trying to tell you something. You have to take the time to remove all the distractions and develop the sensitivity to hear. Don't just remove the distractions, but quiet your mind. Do not let thoughts continue to run in your mind and sit there and respond to them in your head. Quiet your mind. It is like you are trying to tune a radio to that frequency to get that radio station. You don't just pray and walk away. Are you listening? Develop that relationship to tap into that right frequency. Just like the radio station may not play the song that you want to hear when you want to hear it, God may not tell what you want to hear when you want to hear. Realize that God has your best interest at heart. Be honest with yourself.

**He who has ears to hear, let him hear! (Matthew 11:15)**

We want to be able to hear. We need to hear what God is saying. We need to know what the Spirit of God is trying to tell us. Seeking God first can help us to get His guidance on what and how things need to be presented, when to speak, and when you need to be quiet. Just as Nehemiah sought God for help, you can do the same.

**"Now these are Your servants and Your people, whom You have redeemed by Your great power, and by Your strong hand.Lord, I pray, please let Your ear be attentive to the prayer of Your servant, and to the prayer of Your servants who desire to fear Your name; and let Your servant prosper this day, I pray, and grant him mercy in the sight of this man." For I was the king's cupbearer. (Nehemiah 1:10-11)**

It will be God's will for you to be effective at communicating.

**Let your speech always be with grace, seasoned with salt, that you may know how you ought to answer each one. (Colossians 4:6)**

There are times that God will need to speak. He will need a mouthpiece, or shall I say a vessel to use, to send the message. As your relationship develops with God, you may find Him using you. I pray that this letter will be of help. There will be times you will want to be the person that everyone comes to for advice. It no longer has to be about your thoughts and opinions, but it can be the wisdom that God gives you to share with others. He gave wisdom to King Solomon to rule.

> And all the kings of the earth sought the presence of Solomon to hear his wisdom, which God had put in his heart. (2 Chronicles 9:23)

## WRAP UP

As many would take the time to craft an email that would go out to an important audience, you would want to craft what you are saying and how you are saying it in your presentation. Again, how important is it to you? What value do you have on the relationships you have, such as your husband, boyfriend, co-worker, children, family, friends, neighbors, and others?

As the walls to Jericho were brought down, maybe we can get another miracle to take place with the walls coming down that have been put up in your relationships. At the same time, open the lines of communication. ALL THINGS ARE POSSIBLE WITH GOD.

A big value can be placed on the audiences in our life that we encounter. We can look at what is being said and how it is being delivered. The communication can be direct in a sense of working together removing distractions and getting to a common goal. Not direct in a way of being frank or blunt. Speak to the person directly without speaking to others. Don't make any assumptions about anything, but communicate everything. We cannot assume everyone thinks the same as we think or that they communicate in the same way that we would communicate. We want to be simple and clear with our message. As we are communicating, we can keep this Scripture in mind:

> Let no corrupt word proceed out of your mouth, but what is good for necessary edification, that it may impart grace to the hearers. (Ephesians 4:29)

I know that I ask for a lot and bring up many topics. Hang in there and bear with me. Let us move on to the next chapter.

# 4
## HONOR

When I think about honor in the sense of relationships, I think about a time with my grandmother. It was just over 20 years back. My grandfather, her husband, had just passed about a month earlier. The family was at my grandmother's house visiting. Everyone was on the porch and sitting around and talking. In the middle of all the conversations, my grandmother asked me to help her with the cooler. This will show you some of her personality. I get to the trunk of the car and she insisted on grabbing one end of the cooler and allowing me to get the other end. She did not ask one of the other men (my cousins or uncles) to assist me and allow *us* to move the cooler. Instead, she insisted on getting one side while I got the other side. That cooler was heavy with water, ice, and drinks still floating inside. She handled her side like a trooper and did not skip a beat. After the heavy cooler had been placed to the side, my grandmother began to wash my grandfather's brand-new Lincoln right there in front of everyone.

I only had the opportunity to wash it once, when my grandfather was in town with his Lincoln enjoying his new car. He told me to get behind the wheel and start it up. I started the car and then he came over next to me and said, "You can't hear the engine running, can you?" I told him, "No." I could not hear the engine at all, and the car was so quiet. I went ahead and washed my grandfather's car like it was my own.

Now this is a major change of events to see my grandmother with the new Lincoln. It did not feel right to sit there and watch her wash the car. I told her I would wash the car and that she did not have to worry about the car. She found something else for me to do and she continued to wash the car. I said okay, but in my mind, I was thinking she was being stubborn. She finished washing the car and the different family members left for the day to travel back to their homes.

Not long after that day, I came across a Bible passage that spelled out some things to me. I had an encounter with God over what happened. The verses were in Proverbs 31, which talks about a virtuous woman.

> The heart of her husband safely trusts her, so he will have no lack of gain. She does him good and not evil all the days of her life. Proverbs (31:11-12)

My grandfather has passed and is no longer here. God was showing me that the reason my grandmother was washing the car was because she was honoring my grandfather. He kept the car nice and clean and she was continuing to do the same. She was still honoring him in <u>the days of her life</u> even after his death. God was telling me that there is a reason why she is doing what she is doing, and it is not like she will come right out and tell me why. God also said there is another thing. Stop calling her stubborn!

Many people can try to walk things out as an attempt to be in line with the Bible states. They will try to live up to what the Bible tells them to do. My grandmother would live her life day to day. Anyone would be able to see that her lifestyle already lines up with what the Bible teaches. She would just so happen to be doing the right things already. It is like she is hard wired that way. Even after washing the car, she continued to find other ways to honor my grandfather. She would continue to tell us things along the lines of the family name stood for something good and that we needed to be sure that it stayed that way. She continued to do my grandfather good all the <u>days of her life</u>. Not just his. Regardless of how she was treated, she still would be the same. Regardless of what was going on around her, she would remain the same.

There was a Mother's Day a few years later that the family came to celebrate and honor my grandmother. It was decided that after church services, we would meet and have dinner at one of the local restaurants. I remember tables being put together because our family made up a large group. When we all came in and sat together, my grandmother was going to pray over the food. What was different about this was she had us all stand up and hold hands, as we were the largest group centered in the middle of the restaurant in front of everyone. As she began to pray out loud in front of everyone, I looked around and saw the families at the other tables. I saw fathers addressing their children, telling them to be quiet and sit still. "She is over there praying," they would say. My grandmother took charge of the restaurant and she did not have to worry about any misbehavior from her family or any other family in the restaurant.

Some things came naturally to my grandmother. As I said, it seemed that she was hardwired that way. When looking at the course of her life, it helps me to understand it more. An old saying that was mentioned to me before: you can carry the Bible for a long time, but you will find the Bible begins to carry you. It can carry you in your everyday life. Everything from decisions made, how to improve, or even how to help others.

Today, my grandmother is 97 years young. Everyone in her city and my city are currently being quarantined due to COVID-19 (Coronavirus). My grandmother is good, but only the caregivers can see her at the current time to take precautions. She lives alone and has three daughters and a son that are part of her caregiving team. She still has a sharp mind. It's hard to believe that she still has her driver's license. Even over the time of her life, we can see how she honored her husband her family and honored God.

> Charm is deceptive, and beauty is fleeting; but a woman who fears the Lord is to be praised. Honor her for all that her hands have done, and let her works bring her praise at the city gate. (Proverbs 31:30-31)

Women can go out week to week to dress themselves from head to toe. They can get their hair done every week, have the top education, have the best of the best of everything. When all these things fade away, what would be left? From time to time, we will need to make an evaluation of ourselves. What things are more important? What are things that could last a lifetime? What could be passed down to the next generation?

## RESPECT

Contrary to popular belief, one of the most important things for a man is to be respected. I know many people will say that it would be sex. The man may even tell you himself that sex is the most important. If you see the wrong man get disrespected, you will find out very quickly how important it is to him that he is respected.

A study was conducted with 400 men. The question was asked if they would rather be loved or single and respected. Almost 75% of the men that participated in the study would rather be single and respected than be in a relationship. This is not a small topic, so do not just blow this off as if it is something that does not matter. This statistic should show you what respect can do in your relationship and what can occur if it is not in your relationship. There are many men that have suffered things due to respect. Some men are behind bars spending jail time because someone was disrespectable. Some may have negative records because of actions taken when disrespected. There are some that are in a grave today over the need that they have of being respected. Yes, there are some that will go to the grave defending their honor, just to show you how important it is to the man to be respected. Now that you are aware of this fact, I would encourage you to supply this need. Please do not use this against the man. That would only make matters worse.

It's not good to single him out to make him the bad guy, to have all fingers pointed at him and tell everyone all the things that he has done wrong, to build such a strong case against him that has everyone looking down on the man. But wait, you left out the things that *you* did, actions that *you* have taken. That part seems to be left out of the conversations. After the man has suffered all the consequences and everyone has "taught him a lesson," he loses respect. Do you really expect him to have the same respect for you that he once had before?

Now an apology comes after the fact. After the consequences, loss of respect from the group, and other negative occurrences due to the issue. Then the "I am sorry" comes only with a comment behind it to say, "I only did that because you did this." That is not even an apology. You are trying to give an excuse.

Be careful with these types of actions. The reason why I say that is because someone that knows the truth is watching you the entire time. They know the truth and see how the man is being mistreated. They know about the parts of the story that you left out in all those conversations that have taken place. The actions and choices that you make affect more than just you. Your best friend's boyfriend will not commit and get married. He may know the truth about your situation and realize that you are the company that she keeps. The next generation can plan their choices for the future and base them on what they see you do. It is not just about you. Others are watching.

You might be saying, "He is not respecting me. Why should I do that for him?" We all must start somewhere. If we want to get respect, we can start by giving some.

## DON'T CHASE MEN

I know it has been said that a woman should not be chasing a man. Unfortunately, she *is* chasing the man. She is chasing the man away with her actions of dishonor without being aware. When a man is trying again and again and nothing that he is doing is ever enough. The complaints still come in no matter what he does. No appreciation for what he has done. This can make things appear as if he has not done anything and make him feel disrespected.

This can drive a man to go to places that he should not go. The sad thing about it is that the places that the man would be driven to will be places that people would accept him and give him respect. The woman would wonder why he is not coming home. Whenever he is home, he is feels rejected, left out, and unwelcomed. Not appreciated, but simply tolerated.

The bars welcome him with open arms. The bartender and others accept him and fellowship with him in a negative way with no problem. There was a time that he was in a hurry to get a haircut and to get other things done. Now he does not bother to even make an appointment. He can sit in the barbershop all day long just to hang out because of the atmosphere. He was looking forward to coming home to see you, but things are different now. Instead of leaving early because of plans that he had to surprise you, he is volunteering to work longer hours at the job. He's willing to work overtime. The money may be needed. It may not be needed. He may feel more respected on the job than with you. Appreciated for the extra effort and the value that he adds to the company. Even a waiter or waitress can show appreciation for a tip that is left for a dinner that is purchased. The night club will look forward to seeing him. The group at the pool hall will be glad to have him come through and shoot a few games, even if their intentions are not good.

What can make matters worse would be the man going to a strip club. The workers there would make him feel very welcomed. Yes, the bad boys will be there showing off the money they have or pretend to have to impress everyone. The workers here are skilled in getting the man to spend his money. Everyone from the bartender and waitress down to the entertainment. Outside of the bad boys, it may be surprising to find the number of men that are there that had an argument with their girlfriend or wife just earlier that day before coming. You would not want the person that overheard you complaining about him to come across this man's path at this point. The swine that was mentioned in the earlier chapter and the things that they do. This does not give the man an excuse for all the things mentioned; I'm only pointing out the different things that could happen, the different ways that this man can be tempted. These temptations can be prevented if you can handle your conflict differently. Stop saying you do not care. Because YOU DO!

He should not have to go to other places outside of his current relationship to be accepted and respected. None of places mentioned should ever be able to outdo what he has at home. Others can do things for their own advantage. When the words of encouragement and warm welcome come from those in the home, they will come from the heart, not a wrong motive. When others outside of the home are doing things with negative motives, they are not only taking from the man, they are taking from the home.

## HE IS WHERE HE IS BECAUSE OF ME...

I have heard this statement all too often. The woman would complain about the man and then say, "He is where is now because of me." There is more truth behind this statement than one may realize. It's as if they would take pride in what they have done or the influence that they have made in the person's life. As if no one would know where this person would not be if they did not listen to everything that you mentioned. Look at the places that he shops now. Look at how he dresses now. He attends different functions now. He is around different people now. Some woman would say, "That is all because of me." Be careful about this attitude. If there was a chance that you would lose him for any reason, you would be even more upset.

Is it possible that God may have had something to do with some of the good things that are taking place? Can God get some credit? Is it all about you? If you were to lose him, would you be upset to lose him or would you be upset about losing all the work that you put into trying to change him. Is it more of him that you love or is it fear of your work in changing him going to someone else?

Seek God first. Look at some of the tips in the communication chapter on communicating with God. Let God lead you in your interactions with the man. Let God do the work. Let Him operate through you. You will find out the work is not that hard. God would be the one that would be doing the work. Jesus even said His yoke was easy and His burden was light.

**For My yoke is easy and My burden is light. (Matthew 11:30)**

There is a story of a couple that was driving after dinner. The couple had been married for quite some time. They had been together since they were in high school. The couple comes up to a gas station and the husband gets out to pay for the gas to fill up the car. When he gets up the counter, he notices that the clerk was an old classmate. If fact, the clerk dated his wife back when they were all in high school. He says hello to the clerk, made small conversation to catch up a bit and to verify that was the person that went to high school with him and his wife.

He did not gloat in front of the clerk, but he did mention to the wife that her old boyfriend is a clerk at the gas station. He went on to say that if you would have chosen him over me, imagine how your future would been. The husband was able to say this in much confidence. After all, he got the girl and they got married. They are successful, according to everyone else: nice house, nice car, and a nice family. The husband is a CEO of a Fortune 500 company. The wife responded, "If I was married to him, *he* would be the CEO of a Fortune 500 company and I would be in this car with him instead of you."

Not to say that the wife did not play an important role in the husband's life in this example. I am sure she is an intricate part of his success; however, this still comes across as if "he is where is now because of me." It has the type of attitude that he would not be capable of doing anything without her helping. In reality, we all are not capable of doing anything without God. Again, there may more truth behind this statement than she is aware.

The destiny that God may have for the husband could have been different. What some may call success can be something totally different in God's eyes. There are talents and abilities that have been placed in the husband in this example. The husband could have been gifted to communicate with different people from different cultures and backgrounds. Instead of the God-given gifts being used for the destiny that God may have designed for the husband, they were used to become a CEO. God may have intended for the husband to be a person that would have an impact across the world, speaking to leaders, kings, and prime ministers, bringing peace. He could have been called to make changes to help people across the globe.

He is not where God may have intended for him to be and is extremely limited in the things that he can do compared to the destiny God has for his life. This was all limited because it was more glamorous to be a CEO of a Fortune 500 company. He is limited to the offices and places of business to have an influence with those in the company or those that he conducts business with on a regular basis.

He was created to have an influence on people around the world but can only work with those that are in his circle. So yes, he is where he is because of where they wanted him to be in his life. May not have even considered where God wanted the husband to be in his life at this point. Something to think about.

> "For my thoughts are not your thoughts, nor are your ways my ways," says the Lord. (Isaiah 55:8)

God's thoughts are different on what we may call success. God would see success in a different light. He would see you successful with you doing His will by you fulfilling His purpose for your life. When you find it, you will be happy with what you are doing. You will find yourself operating in the talents that He has given you. People will be searching to find you to help them with the projects that they are working on to get your expertise. You may not even look at what you're doing as work because you are operating so well in your gifts and talents. Nothing like fulfilling your purpose and doing what you love.

> **And he said to him, "Well done, good servant; because you were faithful in a very little, have authority over ten cities." (Luke 19:17)**

If you are faithful over a little, God will make you ruler over much. As you are working and developing in your relationships, this will help to put you in a good position for God to bless what you are doing. As you can be supportive, encouraging, or even at times pushing him into his destiny, you can find yourself managing more than you thought that you would. You would see firsthand how the pillow talks and conversations that took place here and there actually manifest into something greater than what you were talking about. The servant in the Scripture was told to have authority over ten cities. What is that compared to running businesses, managing real estate properties, or even being a first lady? All things can be possible when you are carrying out the things that God has planned. When you are conducting yourself in the role that God has called you to play, you are placing yourself in position. You can find yourself doing things easily that others said could not be done. The reason that it could not be done for them is because they tried to do it in their own strength. They left God out of the equation.

## GETTING A RETURN ON WHAT YOU ARE SOWING

How you are treating him can be a direct reflection on what you are receiving from the person. That can be good or bad. If you tell everyone he is not a man, then do not be surprised if he is not a man when you really need him to be a man. Let me ask you a question: Are you saved and have you invited Jesus Christ into your heart? Are you righteous now in God's eyes? If you invited Jesus into your heart, the answer should be yes. The reason you can say this is because God said that you are righteous (speaking in general).

So, in the same regard, God said that the man is the head. What if you treated him that way? God said that he was the head. Not when we felt that he is the head. Not when everything was done to our satisfaction. He is the head when God said he was the head. Just as you would walk out the fact that you are saved and righteous, and you conduct yourself that way. In the same fashion, you can treat the man like the head. Not as a dictator or ruler over everything, but allowing him to take his place. What if you took this action as an act of faith?

**For the husband is head of the wife, as also Christ is head of the church; and He is the Savior of the body. (Ephesians 5:23)**

What if he was treated that way and then suddenly everyone can start to see him begin to take on the traits as the head? What if he started to take on more responsibilities as he has a clearer vision of seeing himself in the role as the head? You'd begin to see the fruit of the head come forth in his life. We would probably say this should have been done earlier. You would have seen the fruit sooner. Just as you can trust that God will complete the work that He has started in your life, you can believe that God can complete the work in the man's life. You might be saying, "It is taking too long. I am not seeing anything." Well, it takes time for you to change, so it will take time with him. The main thing is not to speak against what God has started. If this is a desire that you want from the man, why not sow it into the man? Then reap the fruit that would become of what was sown.

I was working a job, and one day, some coworkers were beside my desk talking while I was working. The conversation really caught my attention. One mother was speaking about her daughter going to a birthday party over the weekend. To my amazement, she said she asked her husband if they had anything in the budget for them to go to the birthday party. He told her they had about $100. She said she took the money and started searching coupons and sales to see what all she could do. I was in awe. She did not complain about the $100. Most people would say, "What am I going to do with $100?" She took it and worked with it without any complaints. This gets even better. She took her daughter to the store with her coupons. There was a sale taking place at the store when they arrived. To make a long story short, she bought the birthday gift and purchased some shoes for her and her daughter. Her husband would be running behind going to work in the mornings, so she bought him some wrinkle free shirts to save some time with the morning rush to work. What really stands out to me is that she did not just spend all the money on herself. EVERY PERSON IN THE HOUSE RECEIVED SOMETHING. She had some thought behind what she got for her husband, and she still provided a birthday gift.

The questions will come from the woman to ask, "Do you like my hair that was just done?" "Do you like my new outfit?" "Do you like my nails?" You can get a straight face from the man and he can say, "That is nice." If the family is over extended and this is over the budget, he has no reason to like the dress or the outfit.

You cannot constantly build a case against the man with all fingers pointing at him and go on and on about what he is doing wrong and complain about what he is not doing—only to leave out everything that you did that was wrong. Like he is the only one that is in the wrong in anything and everything. This is spreading discord. After all this is done, you really expect that the man would still have the same level or respect for you. A better approach would be to save money for the household, not spending everything that is in the household. You can show the steps and sacrifices that you are making to add value to the household.

Often, they can wait for the man to suffer the consequences and then come back and apologize after the fact, only to say, "The only reason I did this is because you did that." Or say, "I am sorry, but..." This is not even an apology. This is not showing honor or respect to the man in any way. It is an approach to make you feel better about what you have done; however, the damage has been done to the man. The hurt is still there, and this has an impact on the relationship. He may not come right out and say it. You cannot make him out to be the bad guy to put yourself on a pedestal. You cannot always play the victim and blame the man. This is spreading discord. Leaving out the details on the part that you played would be the same as a lie. These are part of the six things that the Lord hates. It is part of God's Word.

> **These six things the Lord hates, yes, seven are an abomination to Him. A proud look, A heart that devises wicked plans, Feet that are swift in running to evil, A false witness who speaks lies, and one who sows discord among brethren. (Proverbs 6:16-19)**

When you take the ownership of the part that you played, admit to the actions that you have taken. He would have more respect for you. When the shouting comes down from the mountaintops about him and the wrong that he has done, that causes an issue when there is no mention of the wrong actions that you have taken. Everyone would form a negative opinion about him that remains. It is like he does not even get a chance to redeem himself. Those negative things hang over him from that point forward.

## LEAH

When thinking of someone as an example in the Bible, I think about Leah. Her father was taking advantage of Jacob. Jacob had an agreement to work for Leah's father for seven years in order to marry Leah's sister Rachel. Jacob worked seven years and Laban tricked him by getting Jacob drunk and giving him Leah in marriage. After Jacob found out that he had Leah and not Rachel, he confronted their father, only to be told that he was to marry the oldest daughter first. Jacob had to work another seven years for Rachel.

Leah was in a situation in which she did not have any control. She still had honor for Jacob. She did not ask to be married to this man, but still honored him. God's Word said that Jacob even loved Rachel more than Leah. While she still honored him, God could see that Leah wanted to be loved. Even though things were not going as well as Leah would have liked for them to be, she still put herself in a position for God to move on her behalf.

> Then Jacob also went in to Rachel, and he also loved Rachel more than Leah. And he served with Laban still another seven years. When the Lord saw that Leah was unloved, He opened her womb; but Rachel was barren. So Leah conceived and bore a son, and she called his name Reuben; for she said, "The Lord has surely looked on my affliction. Now therefore, my husband will love me." (Genesis 29:30-32)

In the last moments of Jacob's life, he is speaking a blessing over his twelve sons. He blesses each one individually. After he blesses them, he commands them where he wants to be buried. What I find to be interesting is that the Rachel is not mentioned. He loved Rachel more than Leah at one point, but the fact that she is not even mentioned here tells me things have changed. He commanded them personally to bury him with Leah his wife, just as his fathers were buried with their wives.

> Then he charged them and said to them: "I am to be gathered to my people; bury me with my fathers in the cave that is in the field of Ephron the Hittite, in the cave that is in the field of Machpelah, which is before Mamre in the land of Canaan, which Abraham bought with the field of Ephron the Hittite as a possession for a burial place. Here they buried Abraham and Sarah his wife, there they buried Isaac and Rebekah his wife, and there I buried Leah. The field and the cave that is there were purchased from the sons of Heth." And when Jacob had finished commanding his sons, he drew his feet up into the bed and

breathed his last, and was gathered to his people. (Genesis 49:29-33)

## ABIGAIL

Another woman that comes to mind as an example in the Bible would be Abigail. She happened to be in a unique situation; however, it was different from the situation that Leah encountered. Abigail was described as a beautiful and intelligent woman. She was married to a man named Nabal who was described as a person of harsh and evil doings.

King David had his men next to Nabal's servants while they were shearing the sheep. This is a process that the wool would be cut off the sheep to sell and to take the heavy wool off the sheep to keep them from overheating. David's men were exceptionally good to Nabal's servants, so David sent some messengers to Nabal on the feast day to be included with what was going to be provided to his servants. Nabal had harsh words to the messengers in his response to them.

When the messengers got word back to David, he gathered a large number of men to go back with him to avenge himself for what Nabal did in return for his servants being treated well by David's men. Even though Nabal was evil, disrespectful, and unthankful, Abigail was still being honorable being married to this man.

Abigail went before David and brought food and wine for David and his men. She was very humble and asked for David to overlook the actions of her husband. She knew that David was going to bring harm to her entire household, but Abigail was a peacemaker. She was able to approach David and his men in the way that the first group of messengers should have been approached. This prevented her home from danger. This not only helped her household, but it also helped David.

Abigail did not go back and tell everyone in the town about what she did or how she had to save the day. It was not all about her. She did what was best for all and did not try to put the spotlight all on herself. After everything was said and done, her character was shown. It even caused her to be remarried after her husband died. Regardless of how bad and evil the husband was, Abigail still showed honor. She did not go against Nabal.

> Then David said to Abigail: "Blessed *is* the Lord God of Israel, who sent you this day to meet me! And blessed is your advice and blessed are you, because you have kept me this day from coming to bloodshed and from avenging myself with my own hand. For indeed, as the Lord God of Israel lives, who has kept me back from hurting you, unless you had hurried and come to meet me, surely by morning light no males would have been left to Nabal!" So David received from her hand what she had brought him, and said to her, "Go up in peace to your house. See, I have heeded your voice and respected your person." Now Abigail went to Nabal, and there he was, holding a feast in his house, like the feast of a king. And Nabal's heart was merry within him, for he was very drunk; therefore she told him nothing, little or much, until morning light. So it was, in the morning, when the wine had gone from Nabal, and his wife had told him these things, that his heart died within him, and he became like a stone. Then it happened, after about ten days, that the Lord struck Nabal, and he died. (1 Samuel 25:32-38)

## WRAP UP

The Proverbs 31 woman's character is what is seen and appreciated, not the control that she claims to have over him. I would encourage you to be that woman that would honor God and her husband. Seek God about how to interact with your man. Let God show you how to interact in all your relationships. Reading His Word would be a good start. As you show honor to others and do things God's way, God can see your situation and begin to honor you as He did Leah and Abigail.

The man would want someone who would represent him even if

he is not present at the moment. Making decisions that he would make and doing things the way he would have them done. This would be for the things that he is to be watchful over. I know that are times that he would not be present and a decision would have to be made. Be the person that he safely trusts in that would do him good all the days of her life.

## 5
## COME OUT FROM AMONG THEM

You are unique and wonderfully made. When you are doing what everyone else is doing, your uniqueness can not come forth. Don't be a copy of them. As a younger person, you would do that to try to fit in with the crowd. As you grow older, you want to be different. Here is a good first step: COME OUT FROM AMONG THEM.

When you are the person that God created you to be, you are able reach the destiny God intended for you to have at a faster pace. The talents and gifts can come forward in a sharper manner. The relationships would have more purpose. You can be the wife that has been specifically designed by God for that husband, or if you are not married, your future husband. That position with a company, that book to be written, business to start, taking that role with a family or starting one.

### PEER PRESSURE

Pressure can come on youth as well as adults. The feelings can come as if someone is trying force you to become something that you are not. What makes a bad situation worse is when both people in the relationship will go to or keep the wrong company. There could have been an argument or, shall we say, a disagreement. Both people could be upset with each other. Then each one goes to the wrong friends. The woman will go her friends, relatives, or friend-enemies, and they all give her bad advice out of their bitterness toward someone else in their past. They will say, "You don't need that." "You don't have to put up with that." "You can do better." "You need to get someone else."

The man can go to his wrong friends, co-workers, and relatives and they give him bad advice. "Man. Forget that girl." "Let's go out to the party!" "Forget about her." "Let's get in this club and get on these women up in there!" "Forget that girl!" "We are going to get your mind off of her."

**Do not be deceived: "Evil company corrupts good habits." (1 Corinthians 15:33)**

As the saying goes, "You become what you hang around the most." If the people you are around are not going anywhere, change the company that you keep.

I am glad someone loved me enough to reach out to me to help me stay on track. There was a coworker on my part-time job that I had in high school. She was old enough to have been my mother. Her daughter was in high school at the same time as my older brother. We both lived in the same neighborhood. One night, my coworker spoke to me to give me some advice. She said that she was with her husband eating some breakfast and she saw two young guys sitting in the next booth. One of them was very loud and outspoken and was negative and the other one was nice. The negative one was cussing and was loud and did not even love himself. The other one was nice and kept trying to change the subject. When she got to the end of her story, she said, "You have to watch the company that you keep."

After speaking with her, I was in deep thought. When I thought about what she was saying, it was like it came to me suddenly. She was talking about me! I was leaving a club when they were closing things down. I saw one of my friend's cousins at the club. I knew he got in trouble. All the time. "Let me grab him," I thought to myself. "This will be at least one day he will not get in trouble. He will be with me, so he will not get in any trouble." I told him, "Come with me. I will give you a ride." We stopped at the Waffle House to get something to eat. That was when I saw the coworker and her husband. They were up early with the roosters to eat breakfast. We were out late into the night and still had not made it home. Yes, he kept going on and getting into different tangents. I was trying calm him down. I truly hope that he is all right today. My coworker must have thought that I had forgotten about that morning eating breakfast. I am thankful that she mentioned it to me, along with her advice. I knew her heart was in the right place.

> **He who walks with wise men will be wise, But the companion of fools will be destroyed. (Proverbs 13:20)**

I have found this to be true time and time again. The company that you keep does have an impact on your future. It is a good idea to be around people that are smarter than you. When you think about this concept, you can picture a group of girls that are friends that come together on a regular basis. You can say that they grew up together, so they have known each other for a long time.

The group of friends would come to eat dinner at a restaurant and find that they like the restaurant with all it has to offer. The group decides to meet and have dinner at this restaurant once a month to keep in touch. They have agreed that once a month or more, they would put everything aside and meet. They are all young adults in their early 20s, so this more than reasonable.

As time goes by, the group of friends continues to meet. They are there for each other through the ups and downs of life. They would run in the same circles of people and talk about them when they met. As they spend time together, they begin to form the same opinions and start to think alike. Five years later, you do not see much of a change. They look the same, continue to do the same things, and have the same interests. Jobs may have changed and a few of them might have worked at the same job through the connections that have been made. They may have been in and out of some relationships.

Another 5 years go by and there is a small child at the table. Another person is about to get married, the other just had a recent divorce. Single people in the group start to put more focus on their career and they are not at all the social events like they once were in the past.

Now 15 years have gone by. The divorced person is bitter, so she poisons everything for everyone else. The child is older now and is being impacted by the conversations that are taking place. The career women are in higher positions, but they are lonely and getting advice from the group when they can come together. When someone thinks highly of a person, someone in the conversation can always seem to find something wrong with the person.

In this scenario, it seems that the people in this group can only go so far. It is like they are limited for some reason by a glass ceiling. The reason that occurs is because they are doing everything in their own abilities. They have not considered to do things God's way. God is only an afterthought, meaning they think about Him *after* they get into trouble. They think about Him *after* everything gets hard. If they can think about God and His advice as they did for advice of the group, I wonder where they would be today. God's Word states:

> **That you do not become sluggish, but imitate those who through faith and patience inherit the promises. (Hebrews 6:12)**

It will be better to get the advice from someone that is doing it God's way. This would mean the person is staying consistent. You do not have to consistently do the same things that everyone else is doing. Again, you can live and move with a purpose. A God-given purpose. Follow the person that inherited the promises. Advice can sound good at a moment in time. Things can even look good for a moment in time. Over time, you will see the fruit of that advice that sounded so good. When the dust settles, God's Word will be what stands.

> There is no wisdom or understanding Or counsel against the Lord. (Proverbs 21:30)

The strong women that I have seen over the years would practice the godly approach. They did not run to a circle to gossip and vent about all their problems. They run to God in prayer. They do not confess the wrong or bad things about their family, boyfriend, or husband, saying something negative continually. The strong women that I have observed would make positive declarations over those with whom they are in close relationships. The strong women that stand firm in prayer and with the positive confessions until they see it come to pass.

Let me make my point here: you cannot pray for something or someone and then run to the gossiping table and speak against everything that you just prayed. That is cancelling out everything that you just prayed. It may seem longer and harder, but the return is far greater than the temporary gratification. Do not settle for the temporary thrill of dominating a conversation. Do not try to one-up the other people in the conversation, making a negative confession over a person or a situation.

I spoke with a supervisor at a call center that had an issue with one of his employees. It is amazing how people will try to show off in front of others to no avail. The supervisor was asking a young lady to reach out and ask for help from others if she found that she was would be on a call for a long period of time. This was a call center that constantly ran reports on the calls that were taken. There were goals for the different teams to meet. One of the main goals would be for short call times. Shorter call times would allow more calls to come to the call center, so the long call times would make the team look bad. The employee replied that there were not any issues with their time. The employee continued to be very vocal about the issue. The young lady tried to go over the supervisor's head and attempt to get the supervisor in trouble by telling someone else in management. Unfortunately, the person she spoke with reported to her same supervisor.

Long story made short, the employee continued to be disrespectful in front of her coworker. Things finally got to the point that the supervisor stated that she needed to turn in her badge. She was given chance after chance during this conversation. She wanted to be sure that she got in the last word. On her way out of the door, she mentioned that her boyfriend would be coming to that building and she was to tell him about what all has happened. After she left, the coworker tells the supervisor that the employee that was dismissed was the same person that hit the supervisor's truck in the parking lot. If he were to look at his truck, he would find a dent. Apparently, this was done in the past and they kept it away from that supervisor. I found it interesting that the audience that the dismissed employee was trying to show off by being disrespectful was the same audience that told everything that she was trying to keep a secret. I am glad that the coworker did not bow down to the peer pressure to seem as if they had to act in the same way and be disrespectful. It would have probably caused the coworker to lose their job, as well.

## HABITS AND LIFESTYLES OF OTHERS

They seem to have all the fun. Look at what they are doing. Look at where they live and what they are driving.

This seems to be the latest style or trend. Do not do things just because you see so many others doing the same. You are the leader. You do not have to follow them in what they are doing. At times, people try so hard to stand out from the crowd. This would be a simple way to stand out. I remember telling my niece once in the past, "You do not try to fit in. You set the trend. You do not have to do what everyone else is doing just because it is popular." The same still goes here for youth and adults.

I had a friend that was living with me for a short time. I was helping him out with his current situation. He had a car that was really customized. It was a very loud purple color paint job. The paint looked new. It had custom reams with custom seats with a white and purple interior to match. The two front seats had small televisions in the back of the head rest. This car could be seen from a distance. The car got a lot of attention. The children in the neighborhood keep staring at the car while it sat in my driveway.

One Saturday afternoon, I was sitting out on my porch. It was a spring day with nice weather, so it was like everyone was out and about. I had a function at the church that I was to volunteer for in a few hours. As I was sitting there on my porch, there seemed to be so many women that were driving by in such a short about of time. They would look at the car and look at me. They would look at the car and look at me. The feeling made a single man want to stay out on the porch a little longer, but I know that I had somewhere to be. I know things like this make you feel that you are missing out on something, but often times, being where you are supposed to be can keep you out of a lot of trouble. I always thought about that with King David not being on the battle lines where he should have been, but he was watching Bathsheba take a bath on the roof top. I left and went to the function that I was to volunteer to work.

The function went well; however, when I got home, God began sharing some things with me. He was like, "Okay, Mr. Big Shot. Did you think about all of the ladies that were driving by? Did you notice what they were attracted to? Did you take a close look at them? What were they driving? Where were they coming from or going to?" Things began to make more sense. The ladies driving by were not living the lifestyle that I was living. I could tell from how they were dressed and even from the music they were playing. If I would just focus on what I needed to be focused on, the right person would come in place. I need to get away from those distractions. It was God's way of saying, "You did not miss out on anything." It is funny as I think about this now, because I do not recall that many women driving through the neighborhood since that day. Oh, how a distraction can throw you off track if you will allow it.

## SLEEPING AROUND

In the society today, people are very sexually active. It is portrayed like it is such casual thing because everyone is doing it. Seems like everyone is participating. Just because everyone else is doing this, it does not mean that you have to participate. Just because you have sex with someone or even with many partners, it does not make you a woman. It does not mean that you are grown. This is not an action that should be taken outside of a marriage.

> Now the works of the flesh are evident, which are: adultery, fornication, uncleanness, lewdness... (Galatians 5:19)

The movies that you watch and the social media that you read can make it look like this is normal, that it is okay to have this lifestyle. I can look fun and be portrayed as if you are missing out on something. Two people in a movie would have a scene where they would go into a room alone. Once the sexual activity is completed, one person smokes a cigarette that never smoked before, as if this act causes them to become cool and you should try it sometime. There is more to this than what meets your eyes. There is more that has been transferred that just a sexual encounter.

The interesting thing about it is that the different forms of media do not show you the bad side. The consequences to the actions can come in different ways. Things change after sex is involved. They will not be as they were before. Sexual diseases can be transferred to you. Unplanned pregnancies can occur. Even if you are using protection, there are no guarantees. There are diseases that you can get that don't have a cure. I do not mind missing out on these things with the so-called fun that they are having.

The lie that is being told is that you want to hook up with someone while they are interested. Like having sex with them will be something that will keep them around. If the person will leave over sex, what kind of person are you with anyway? There is not a need to whet an appetite for something that you should not be doing. Do not whet our appetite and cause a desire for something that needs to go unfulfilled. Other lies are for you to test the waters, see how well the person performs, know what you are getting before you commit. These lies can cause you to commit to the wrong person, or even worse, they can cause you to miss out on the right person that God has for you. If you want something different, you must get away from these lies and do something different.

> **Flee sexual immorality. Every sin that a man does is outside the body, but he who commits sexual immorality sins against his own body. (1 Corinthians 6:18)**

I remember a few of the part-time jobs that I had as teenager. Some of the people that I worked with may be alarming to many. Dirty jokes were told. Many sexual references were made. You would have thought the women were offended at the things that were said by others, but they were laughing right with the people telling the dirty jokes. The guys would talk big and say big things when they were around all the fellows. Whenever they would get with me one on one, they would all say nearly the same thing. It would all be along the same lines. The statements would be something like, "Hey, I do not regret having my kids. I wish I would have waited until I was in a better position to take care of them." "It would be best for you to wait." Yes, they talked trash all the time, but they took care of their children.

I remember one of them had a child that was older than I was as the time. Even though I was not in part of everything that they talked about, they were telling me not to do things in the way that they have done in their past. It does not take a lot to come out from among them. I do remember one of them confronting me one night. He was one of ring leaders of the dirty jokes. Just as he was big and bad enough to tell the dirty jokes, he was just as big, just as bad, and just as bold to look at me eye to eye. He told me, "KEEP IT IN YOUR PANTS!" That advice would go right in line with God's Word. That statement came from the right heart.

> Therefore "Come out from among them And be separate, says the Lord. Do not touch what is unclean, And I will receive you." (2 Corinthians 2:17)

The Word of God helps us by providing the guidelines to keep us out of the dangers that the lifestyle can bring. In other words, we can "come out from among them." Keeping yourself for marriage would be something that would always be a help in the long term. Keeping yourself *in* the marriage is even better. We cannot take that part out of the equation, as many people often do. This may be frowned upon by many, but if the person frowns on that, what kind of person are they anyway? If the person cannot respect **that**, then they will not have respect for you in other aspects of the relationship. Keep that in mind. If you want a person with all this experience, wouldn't that mean the person has been with many people before you? What all would that person bring to you? What spirits, diseases, emotional baggage is coming with the package? Has the person addressed any of these issues? All these elements, along with others, are what you can be inviting into you and around you, to be direct about it.

## WALK OF FAME AND WALK OF SHAME

If you are not aware, there is a walk that takes place after an encounter. It is either a Walk of Fame or a Walk of Shame. Not to say that the walks are correct, but it will alert you to the mindset of these that are watching you. We can say that a young lady would go and see a young man and they engage in a sexual encounter. When the man would walk out of the room, he is celebrated. Everyone smiles at him and admires him as if he has conquered something. It would be like a scene when someone scored the winning touchdown at the big football game. Everyone is giving him a high five. Team members jump up with backside going up to touch backside. Team members lift the person that scored the touchdown and marches him across the field. For the man, it would be a Walk of Fame. He is seen in this light because he has scored.

As for the woman, when she walks out of the room, she is not seen in this light. She is looked down upon. The men are wondering what all she has done. They are thinking who will be the next person that will hook up with this woman. The other women would look at her and think, "Oh no, she did not." This woman would not be looked at in the same light. She is frowned upon and looked down upon by others. Not to say that this is right, but the woman is devalued. When the woman walks out, she would be seen as taking a Walk of Shame.

Now, please be careful regarding who you are with behind closed doors. Even if nothing occurs, you must be careful. You can be perceived to have done something and the man can leave that perception right where it is in people's minds. After all, he thinks it will make him look good—at your expense, I might add. Sister, be careful with your decisions. God loves you and I love you. A condom cannot protect your heart.

**Abstain from every form of evil. (1 Thessalonians 5:22)**

Even as children, we would stand together and talk on the corner or take a break from playing. We would see a lady leaving a man's apartment. We would see how the lady's hair would be all messed up. Her hair did not look like that when she went into his apartment. That was a sign for us to know what they were doing. It would be obvious even to us, the children. We were not stupid. It could be seen what was going on. Not to say that this was right in any way, but even as children, we had the same mindset of a Walk of Fame for the man and a Walk of Shame for the woman. It really stood out being that they were not married.

## NIGHT CLUBS

The night clubs are a place that are attended by many. They may think that going to a club would be a place to meet people. Not a good idea. If the person is going there now, they will want to continue going to the club later. Not everyone will attend for that purpose. There are some that attend just to hook up with someone. A lot of this can be like the late-night house parties, which can be more dangerous. Some people can go out to blow off some steam and relax in this way. It may be a celebration and a group of friends may decide to go out together. A group of workers can decide to go out for drinks. All of this can sound so casual, like this is a normal lifestyle and there is nothing wrong with having a little fun. Things can all start off so small and so subtle.

This scene is not as innocent as it may seem. Times in the past, the group would go out and talk about what all happened, who they all saw, and talk about where they were going to go the next time, whether it would be the next day, the next week, or even the next event. You do not know what all is waiting for you, especially this day and time. In the past, the guys would be bragging about how many numbers they got from all the people they met. Now, there are guys and girls taking part of the same challenge. There are some women looking to see who they can get close to turn out, then brag to the men about how many they were able to get. It is not just the men that are trying to hook up. There are some women doing the same.

The ladies looking for Prince Charming will have to be careful also. Some of the men can put on a facade to dress and look as if they are so hard because that is what a woman may be looking for in a man. He can look like he is hard on the outside. The lady can find out later that this person is bi-sexual. This could cause her to be hurt after the fact.

I hate to hear about the stories of things taking place at the late-night house parties. You do not always have security at a house. There have been stories of people attending the parties to find that someone has slipped a drug to them. They were not conscious and did not remember everything that happened. Sad, but it has happened to males and females. I do not advocate alcohol in any way, but if you are drinking anything, you need to see that the seal is being cracked opened that the drink being poured. Alcohol or a soda, it does not matter. Have your eyes open. Keep an eye on your cup and never put it down for any reason. It is safer to stay out of the environment all together.

You would want to keep yourself pure. Places like this would have the wrong spirits along with the company that they keep. These would not be the places that you would want to hang around. Those bad spirits would not be the spirits that you would want to hang around you.

Another lifestyle that occurs would be a couple that would live together without being married. This is not a lifestyle that I would encourage. This can look good at the very appearance. "Hey, we can save money. We will be together. We can share the things that we have." Do not do this without a marriage commitment. You may think this will be a test run to see how it will be once you get married. You have already failed the test. Do you really think you would be in a home together and nothing would happen sexually? Do not put yourself in that situation. If children are involved, that can make things worse. The children can have issues with the mother's boyfriend or with the father's girlfriend. When you are living in this condition, the children can be at risk of be molested. I am not saying that would be the case for everyone that is living this way; however, what I am saying is if the person will not commit to marry you, what commitment do they have for your children? Are you for rent? Are your children for rent? You might be reading this and saying, "You don't understand. We are trying to survive. This person is providing." Do not sell yourself short. If you have Christ in your life, God is your source! Do not make another person your source. If you allow a person to be your source, you give them control over you. My God supplies my need. I would encourage you to put your trust in Him and not in a person.

And my God will meet all your needs according to the riches of his glory in Christ Jesus. (Philippians 4:19)

If you are a giver, you qualify for this verse. You might not have money to give anything. If your heart is really into wanting to give, God will show you something that you can give to a church or a ministry. He will show you how you can give along with different ways that you can give. Not only finances but time, encouragement, or things around your house that you are not using that can be a help to someone else and their family. You will find that God can take care of you a lot better than the person can provide for you. There will be peace with what God provides.

## KNOW WHO YOU ARE

Once you know the will of God, this where faith begins. When you know who you are, as well as your purpose, you will not compromise that for anyone or anything. You will not let the opinions of others sell you short of your God-given destiny. You may say, "My background is not pretty. You do not know where I come from. You do not know what I come from or have been through."

The first order of business is that you came through. Many are still GOING... THROUGH... You do not have to put your identity in your background or anything else. If you have Christ as your Savior, put your identity in Him. When you think about this, you can see yourself as God does. He puts out winners.

You are not a b-----. Stop calling yourself or others by this name. You are not a jump off. You are not a ho. You are not just a baby mama. You are not somebody's flunky. You are not a has-been. You are not like someone's toilet paper to use and be thrown away when they are done using you. You are not a thot. Do not see yourself as any of these things. Do not associate with anyone that would treat you as if you are any of these things that were mentioned.

It is just as important that you respect yourself, not to be treated or mentioned in this manner. Do not treat anyone else in this manner. Do not look down on someone or call them any of the negative things mentioned. I spoke about the media earlier, which would include films, TV, social media, magazines, newspapers, music, and all. Do not participate in anything that would support you being treated negatively in this way. Those companies go off numbers. Do not use your finances to increase their numbers. Even if you look at the blogs or see free videos or materials, the number of hits go up for them to increase and add volume for their content. It is one thing for them to put out material to put you down and present you in a negative way. It is another thing for you to support and use your own money to pay for this to take place. Let us walk in wisdom.

You have a great purpose. You were born for a reason. Regardless of how you got here, you are here for a purpose. Do focus on how you got here, even if it may have been something negative. You are here. You have a purpose. This can be confirmed in God's Word.

**Before I formed you in the womb I knew you: Before you were born I sanctified you; I ordained you a prophet to the nations. (Jeremiah 5:5)**

**For I know the thoughts that I think toward you, says the Lord, thoughts of peace and not of evil, to give you a future and a hope. (Jeremiah 29:11)**

Get yourself in this frame of mind. You will not get tossed to and fro. Be established in who you are and do not compromise to conform to or fit what someone else wants you to be. Be who and what God desires you to be. You stay consistent with this and don't allow anyone to talk you out of what you were created to be.

The media can have a certain image portrayed before you to have you believe that you would have to be a certain way for you to be accepted. God has already accepted you. You do not have to be what they are portraying you should be. Let God's Word be your guide.

The magazines would have the waistline so thin it is not realistic. The software that is used would make a person look so thin, it's not even humanly possible for anyone to achieve what is in the image. The person in the picture would even say, "I wish I could look like that," right along with everyone else.

This type of media would highlight the trends, telling you what fashion to purchase, advice to take, how to wear your hair, and other things to do. Do not let others determine where you are to go or what to do. Let the Bible be your guide. As you have the Bible as your guide, you have the beautiful mind that God has given you to help you make choices in life.

As you seek God first and foremost, you will know. Others can lead you down a path that is for their own benefit and not yours. They can tell you something that is completely wrong and be fully aware, but will tell you what you want to hear in order to get you to participate in the activities that are not good.

> **But seek first the kingdom of God and His righteousness, and all these things shall be added to you. (Matthew 6:33)**

Once you know who you are, you can stand firm. When others are trying to get you to do other things, you can choose not to go. If they decide not to associate with you because you are not doing the things that they do or go to the places that the go, just say, "That's fine." LET THEM GO. You will know that those things will compromise your destiny. I would tell people that you have a higher calling. Do not even worry about those things.

## WRAP UP

With the things that are taking place in society today, I would ask that you not pattern your life after the things that are being portrayed. You have things about you that are different from everyone else. You cannot tap into these things if you conforming to be like everyone else. Your talents and gifts need to come forth. There are others that need what you have. Do not sell them short. We need to hear your voice. We need to read your book. We need to be a patron at your place of business. We need to see your artwork. We need to be moved by your poetry. We need to benefit from your God-given scientific breakthroughs. We need to benefit from your skillset. Come out from among them and take whatever time you need to develop your gifts.

Keep in mind that you do not have to do what others are doing. You do not have to be accepted by them or be included with their group. Come out from among them. You do not have to adopt the lifestyles of others. You do not have to bow down to peer pressure. Look to God to be your source and let Him define you.

# 6
# MANAGE YOUR EMOTIONS

As a child, I grew up with a very vicious dog. He was a pit bull terrier. Some dogs would walk with the owner guiding them with a rope or a leash. The dog was so strong that he was walked on a chain. I should have known that this dog was going to be stronger as he became older. When he was a puppy and we went to pick him out from the older dogs that were around him, they would pull a rope at opposite ends like they were playing tug of war as dogs. When my dad would get a new tire, he would put the old tire in the dog pin. This dog would pick up the tire and sling it when he saw a cat or another dog in the yard and he could not get out of his tall dog pen to go chase after the intruders of his domain. Over time, the tire would be torn apart, believe it or not.

One cold winter night, my dad had the dog come in the house with us. The temperatures were going to drop too low and it would not have been safe for the dog to have been outside in those conditions. My older brother, being devious, pulled out a full-length mirror and put it in front of the dog. He started barking and ran toward the mirror as if he were going to attack the dog that he saw in the mirror. Of course, the dog in the reflection is doing the same thing. My brother moves the mirror as he is laughing at the dog. This big strong dog runs through the hall into the different rooms, frantically looking for the other dog in the reflection. The dog still does not realize that he was himself in the mirror. It was his own reflection.

As funny as this story may be, we would want to look at how the wrong image can bring the wrong emotion. Our dog was big, strong, and powerful. You can see that when all those traits are used in the wrong way, they can cause some serious damage. Not all of the damage can be repaired. Ask me about that night and the next morning. Things were broken that could not be repaired. The dog tore a pair of my jeans apart just like he did the tire. The actions that you take and the things that you say can be actions or statements that hurt others. You cannot take them back. They are not repairable at times because people will not forget. They may forgive you, but they will take precautions with you in the future, if you know what I mean. They can keep you at a distance.

When looking at the history of the pit bull terrier, I found that the breed was used for bull baiting back in the 1800s in the United Kingdom. This was a bloody sport that was later outlawed. This animal was used in this way against an animal that is more than five times his size. Throughout history, this animal has been with bad owners and has received a bad reputation. When the dog is constantly placed in the circumstances like bull baiting or dog fights in pits, and it's not being loved properly, I can understand why the breed is so strong and aggressive. Even though they are strong, they always needed to stick to their strategy. Their very life would depend upon it if they are being baited by a bull. This is still different from the hundred people that we can see running from bulls like we watch on TV. This breed did not have a large space to run or the bull having a hundred of other options to chase down. It makes them aggressive to survive being in the situation that their owner has placed them.

Dogs from this breed have often been handled by bad owners. That is not the case for every owner. There have been videos that you can see members of this breed are not the bad dangerous dogs as many would think. Videos have been published where the dogs are obedient and seen in plain view. The good owner would make a big difference. I saw in one video how a five-year-old girl spread out a bowl of dog food in front of five pit bulls. She kept telling them to wait as she continued to spread out the food from a bowl that was almost as big as her. To my amazement, none of the dogs touched the food until the girl gave the command. After the dogs started eating, the mother turned the camera around and stated, "You just watched a five-year-old command five pit bulls." There are other videos that show dogs of this breed that are not dangerous and aggressive, who are more protective of people and not attacking. You would be able to tell that these dogs were cared for differently. They were loved as a dog should be. They were trained about things that they were not aware. They had a good owner.

If the good owner was God and the bad owner was the devil, which owner could you say you were being directed by when it came to spiritual things? What choices would be made? Would you make the good choices to please God or would you make the wrong decisions that please the devil and others? Can you stay the course regardless of the circumstance or would you adjust because the devil placed a roadblock in front of you? I know it is a lot easier said than done.

I know that there are many that are reading this that are dealing with past hurts from different situations. Maybe you were not loved properly. You may have been abused, molested, abandoned, or not loved at all. Manage your emotions over the hurt. Do not let the pain of the past hurt direct your future. You are an overcomer. You are more than a conqueror.

> You are of God, little children, and have <u>overcome</u> them, because He who is in you is greater than he who is in the world. (John 4:4 *emphasis added)

> Yet in all these things we are more than conquerors through Him who loved us. (Romans 8:37 *emphasis added)

Some things can start off so small and so subtle. Someone can have a bad day and decide to get a drink. As more bad days come, the more the person drinks. Before you know it, the person has a drinking problem. If you can manage the issue of what is causing the bad days, you could prevent the negative things occurring from the bad days.

If you are still harboring hurt from a bad relationship, you would want to get your heart right from that old relationship first. Don't bring the hurt and bitterness to the next one. Work to address things that you can. I know that you are not able to address everything in your own strength. I would encourage you to develop a relationship with God to allow Him to guide you. I have spoken with people that have different challenges and I've seen them turn to different vices during their challenging times. I've seen some go shopping when they are depressed. Some eat more when they are depressed. There was a lady that told me that she gained all her weight when her mother died years earlier. We do not have to do whatever our emotions are telling us. If you can pause, then do so, and get some direction from God in the situation. Let God and the Spirit rule in your heart. Don't just sit back and allow the emotions to take over.

What normally happens is that a situation occurs and someone tries to put you on the spot. Things are rushed and you are pushed in a corner to make a quick decision. You feel so forced to do something. The tactic that the devil would use is to apply pressure along with a pile of distractions to get you off track. Make you feel forced to make something happen. You do not have to bow down to this pressure. Do not let the devil set the pace of what is going on in your life. You set the pace in your life with your faith, not the devil's fear. The athletes in sports know that you do not allow your opponent to take you out of your game. With the help of God, you can set the pace and not allow the wrong approach to cause you to make a bad decision. God's Word says to seek first the kingdom of God.

> **But seek first the kingdom of God and His righteousness, and all these things shall be added to you. (Matthew 6:33)**

Make sure that what you do will be in line with God's Word. The more time you spend with God, the more sensitive you will be to God and His Word. You can walk it out better. If you need wisdom in the situation, you can just ask Him for it before running off and doing everything in your own strength and intellect.

As an example, I remember one time on a rainy day, the storms were bad and the city had flash flood warnings taking place. I was seated at a restaurant after work eating my diner. My phone began to ring. I saw it was my neighbor calling me. In my spirit, God was telling me that a tree has fallen and your neighbor is calling to tell you. I was thinking, "Na. That did not happen." I answered the phone and greeted my neighbor. Everything seemed cool. He said his son called him. I said, "That is good. How is he doing?" Then those words came out of his mouth. "My son said that one of your trees fell. He said cars can still get by, but the tree is in the street." I told him thanks for letting me know.

Thoughts came through about how it looked. What was the damage? I needed to get over there and see what all needed to be done. Then I had a thought that I needed to take control. **No!** I am not getting in my car running frantic across town. I made a few calls about some direction, but that was all. I made the decision to finish eating my meal. I chose to finish my meal and enjoy what I was eating. It was the first Friday of the month. My church normally has a first Friday night service. My original plan was to attend the service. I decided right then and there that I would still attend the church service. I would not allow this circumstance to prevent me from attending the service or from me finishing my meal. My neighbor's son said cars would be able to get by driving on the same street in front of my house. **THE TREE WILL BE THERE WHEN I GET THERE!** I finished my meal and attended the church service as planned. I did not allow the situation to determine what I was going to do.

I got home that night and saw the tree laying down. My neighbor's son was right. Cars were still able to get by. It was a large portion of the tree that fell. If I rushed from the restaurant home, there would not have been much of a difference. The next morning, I begin to work on removing the tree. As I started, others walked by and said it was good that no one got hurt. We counted the blessings in the situation. The neighbors began to come out and help one by one. I was talking to one neighbor about making a purchase of a chain saw, but one of the other neighbors continued to cut off parts of the tree and I was not about to leave her working on my tree while I left to go to the store. What was interesting is that another set of neighbors pulled up with a chain saw. Their young son came along, who I think was eight at the time. He had on a set of work gloves that fit his small hands. They all came ready to help. Another neighbor came that had another chain saw. Within two hours, the fallen tree was cut in small pieces and placed on the side of the road to be picked up. I do not know how I would have done everything without the help of my neighbors.

The issue with the tree was resolved. Panic and worry would not have helped the situation. I had to manage my emotions. Focusing and meditating on negative images was not going to cause a resolution to come to pass. It was a surprise to me, but it was not a surprise to God. God provided all the help and resources needed. God already went before me. There were steps of faith that I had to take. There was not even a cost involved. Now you know I had to give them a **SHOUT OUT!**

I could have had more peace about the situation. I should have known that God would take care of things. I still have more to work on. A better example would be Jesus. With this example, we can see in God's Word how He handled the situation when this tactic was used against Him.

> But Jesus went to the Mount of Olives. Now early in the morning He came again into the temple, and all the people came to Him; and He sat down and taught them. Then the scribes and Pharisees brought to Him a woman caught in adultery. And when they had set her in the midst, they said to Him, "Teacher, this woman was caught in adultery, in the very act. Now Moses, in the law,

commanded us that such should be stoned. But what do You say?" This they said, testing Him, that they might have something of which to accuse Him. But Jesus stooped down and wrote on the ground with His finger, as though He did not hear. So when they continued asking Him, He raised Himself up and said to them, "He who is without sin among you, let him throw a stone at her first." And again He stooped down and wrote on the ground. Then those who heard it, being convicted by their conscience, went out one by one, beginning with the oldest even to the last. And Jesus was left alone, and the woman standing in the midst. When Jesus had raised Himself up and saw no one but the woman, He said to her, "Woman, where are those accusers of yours? Has no one condemned you?" She said, "No one, Lord." And Jesus said to her, "Neither do I condemn you; go and sin no more." (John 8:1-11)

Jesus paused and gave an answer and then stooped down again and wrote on the ground. He set the pace. He did not allow the group to pressure Him or push Him into making a decision. Jesus did not even let it make Him sweat. He still handled the situation. Recognize the tactic that the enemy is using against you.

## CALM YOURSELF

There was a mother that was speaking to me about her daughter years ago. She mentioned that her daughter got pregnant at a young age. She told me about how she began to fuss and fuss at the daughter to the point that she got exhausted. She finally settled down. After she settled down, she began to hear from God. She started to see things from the daughter's perspective. She could then she how scared her daughter was and the help that her daughter would need.

Another point about the importance of managing your emotions is that you would want to position yourself to be able to hear from God. **Calm yourself.** The Scriptures can come to mind. You can begin to get the direction on what to do. You can pray to get the insight and details.

> Call to Me, and I will answer you, and show you great and mighty things, which you do not know. (Jeremiah 33:3)

I had a friend that lived in the neighborhood next to mine. He lived in an apartment with his aunt. When I think of someone that was very calm in a difficult situation, I think about his aunt. His aunt had a baby girl. Her baby passed away the next year after we graduated from school. One Saturday morning, I was over and she shampooed my hair and sat me down and talked to me. As she was drying my hair, she was telling me, "You need to make sure that you are giving God some of your time." I was surprised to see how she was ministering to me with the situation that she was going through. I do not think the child was even a year old, but she was calm and strong. She still took the time to speak an encouraging word to someone else.

We all need to manage our emotions. Do not let your emotions or feelings determine your actions. The emotions can be good or bad. You can still do the wrong things but have good intentions. At the time that I am writing this chapter, it is the day that the funeral for George Floyd is taking place. There were many that gathered for his funeral. George Floyd died at the hands of a police officer and his death was recorded on video. The way that George Floyd died has caused many protests, looting, riots, violence, and buildings being burned across the country. Many of the actions that have been taken since Floyd's death were taken without anyone trying to manage their emotions. Some torched and damaged the same community where they live, being instigated by others outside of their community. I wonder what the outcome would be if they would all put the same effort and energy into building the communities. Not just the buildings, but the people inside. I pray that everyone would take a similar approach in building going forward. Take a moment to get some direction before reacting.

> The simple believes every word, but the prudent considers well his steps. A wise man fears and departs from evil, but a fool rages and is self-confident. A quick-tempered man acts foolishly, and a man of wicked intentions is hated. (Proverbs 14:15-17)

> He who is slow to wrath has great understanding, But he who is impulsive exalts folly. (Proverbs 14:29)

This is a prime example of why we need to seek God first before taking actions. Did your mother ever ask you, "So if all your friends jumped off a bridge, will you jump off the bridge too?" You are jumping off the bridge when you jump into situations without getting all the information before taking actions. You are hurting yourself and you do not realize what you are doing. Calming yourself will help you to manage your emotions. You will be able to remove the distractions. Quiet your mind and you will be better able to hear from God. Trust me. He is trying to talk to you. Don't let your emotions block you from hearing what He is telling you.

> He who is slow to anger is better than the mighty, And he who rules his spirit than he who takes a city. (Proverbs 16:32)

> Whoever has no rule over his own spirit Is like a city broken down, without walls. (Proverbs 25:28)

See that you are the one that is in control, not your emotions. Calm yourself.

## NEVER MAKE A DECISION OUT OF EMOTION

Most bad decisions can be made when people are mad, tired, or in a desperate state. If you find yourself in an emotional state, make your decision at a later time. You will want to get all the information and make a sound decision. I would not want a bad decision to come back to bite you later. Think of when someone gets upset while on a phone call with customer service over the phone. A bill may be higher than normal. A charge can be on the bill that was overlooked. Now that the bill is higher, the person gets upset and says, "Cancel my service." Clearly, they have not thought things through, have not prayed for insight, have not taken ownership of the fact that they overlooked something. When the person has calmed down, they can see where they have made a mistake, but pride kicks in and they blame others. They go to a different carrier and they are now paying more money. Keep in mind that this emotion is temporary. The decision that is made will have a longer impact.

This is something on a smaller scale; however, there are bigger decisions that are made that have a greater impact. Never make a permanent decision off a temporary emotion.

> **While we do not look at the things which are seen, but at the things which are not seen. For the things which are seen are temporary, but the things which are not seen are eternal. (2 Corinthians 4:18)**

Keep this Scripture in mind. It can really show you how temporary the emotion can be when making decisions. At the very time that these things occur, others can be around you that can have an influence on you in the situation. It is none of their business. They make comments. "I know you are not going to take that." "If it was me, I would do this, or I would have done that." It is amazing that people that you do not even know have no problem giving their opinion to get you to do something that does not cost them anything. If you ask them to put their own money where their mouth is, they will get quiet. Do not pay attention to those negative comments. Remove those distractions.

## MEDIA

Do not let the media or others tell you what your option should be. You have your own mind. Monitor the things that you are watching.

When you look at the same things over and over, it is like you are being programmed as to what to watch, what to think, how you are to be, what you are to do. Do not allow others to put words in your mouth. They do not represent you. You need to be the one to represent you. This can be accomplished with you speaking up and supporting those things that support you in a good light.

Popular opinion is not always God's option. As a group's agenda would change, their opinions will change. God does not change. He is the same yesterday, today, and forevermore.

**Jesus Christ is the same yesterday, today, and forever. (Hebrews 13:8)**

Do not let the media or others tell you what your option should be. Not options for yourself or anything else for that matter. God blessed you with your own mind. The best results for you will come from God's Word. That is the stable foundation.

**Humble yourselves in the sight of the Lord, and He will lift you up. (James 4:10)**

The number of likes or dislikes do not determine your value. The number of friends that you have or the number of people that accepted you does not determine your value. Even if you are blocked, it does not determine your value. Find your identity in Christ and walk out the things in the Word of God. Your true value is in God. Keep your focus on what He has created in you. Stop looking at the numbers and using them to determine your self-worth. The numbers you need to look at are the chapters and verses in the Bible. Let God be the one that gets you what you are seeking. It will be the right kind of fame in the right timing with the right people. The lower you get, the higher the plateau He can bring you.

## YOU CANNOT LET EMOTIONS RUN THE SHOW

There are times that you will need to think with your head and not your emotion. It has always been said to follow your heart. Not so! If God's Word says one thing and your feelings are saying something different, stick with God's Word. Do not let your heart or your feelings get you in trouble. Don't let your heart fool you. Do not love the man so much that you are doing the wrong things to try to get him or even keep him.

> **The heart is deceitful above all things, And desperately wicked; Who can know it? (Jeremiah 17:9)**

I had an interesting conversation with a coworker a while back. The discussion that we had was about domestic violence. I understand that there are different reasons why it would be hard to tell a woman to get some help and she will refuse the help. I was speaking with a female and she provided some insight—not that we are experts by any means. I am aware that many cases occur, and the women would remain for different reasons. Some may have self-esteem issues and they will think that they will not be able to do better than they are currently. They may think that no one else would get in a relationship with them, as if this is the only type of person that she would be able to attract. Some women can be in a survival mode. This man is providing what is needed so she remains in this environment because she feels that she needs to survive. If she is to get out of this situation, what will she do? Where can she go? There are women that are also in fear. Fear of what the man will do. There can be fear of all the threats that have been made of what he will do if she leaves. So, this woman remains in the same situation.

I am aware of these types of situations and would say that this is not a healthy situation. There are resources that are available. I would encourage to seek out the resources and speak with those that are knowledgeable about this and are aware of the laws in your area.

Well, getting back to the conversation that I had with my

coworker... We talked about the main items, but I had a question on how can they stay in that predicament? Let us say there is a female that I grew up with from a child. The female has beaten up boys in fights in the neighborhood growing up. This has been seen by many. I went on to tell the young lady that if this person came to me and said that her husband or boyfriend hit her, I would have a problem with them both. I would have a problem with the man hitting her and I would question as to why she let him hit her at all. "Back in the day you, did not let Ray Ray or Pokkie hit you. We all saw how you duked it out with them to the point that Ray Ray and Pokkie learned their lesson and did not bother you anymore after that day. How will you allow anyone else to hit you in any way?"

The young lady responded to me and said, "You don't understand. A woman can still be in love with the person." I have not heard about that part being mentioned up in this type of conversation. I wonder why people do not talk about that part. She went on to say that he could hit the woman and the woman turns around and hits him back. This behavior could continue, but the woman can choose to remain in this situation because she is still in love with this person. That was a point that I did not consider. I could understand that there are different issues regarding domestic violence. I'm sorry that this is occurring. This situation is not healthy. If there are children involved, that will make matters worse. This would cause there to be more victims in the situation. I pray that sisters will get the right kind of help to resolve the situation in the right way. God can give you the desires of your heart. God has not given you the spirit of fear. God will supply all your needs if you are a tither and a giver.

> Take delight in the Lord, and he will give you the desires of your heart. (Psalm 37:4)

> For God has not given us a spirit of fear, but of power and of love and of a sound mind. (2 Timothy 1:7)

> And my God shall supply all your need according to His riches in glory by Christ Jesus. (Philippians 4:19)

There was a young lady that was interested in a young man. She was trying to be with him and was willing to do what she could to be in a relationship with him. Again, she should not be following her heart. She participated in sexual activity with others in hopes to be with this person. When everything was said and done, the young man did not want to be in a relationship with the young lady because she was involved sexually with others. Please be smarter. Think about the Walk of Fame and that Walk of Shame. The man is praised for allowing others to score. The woman is looked down on. Sisters, please be careful and make wise decisions. God loves you, and I love you, too.

The same actions can take place on college campuses. Fraternities, sororities, and other organizations can participate in different activities that can include young men and young ladies doing wrong things, getting involved in different activities to get into the club to be part of the organization. Usually, the person will do whatever is asked because the person wants to get in for desires for fortune and fame, future jobs, stability, and popularity. God is your source. God's Word says that He will make your name great, so He will make your name great. Not the organizations. Find your identity in Christ. You are God's child if you received Christ in your heart. Live your life in a way that God can get the glory. It is not all about us. Do not allow others to pimp you for their gain at your expense. After they finish using you, they will throw you away like a piece of tissue that they are done using.

This will not help. You will leave feeling worse than you did when you started. You are valuable. If no one has told you that, let me be the first. You are God's creation. He would not create something or someone that did not have worth. He created the entire earth so that you would have a place just before He placed you in it. He also created us all in His image. Do not sell yourself short to be in the club. You do not have to compromise your morals or your beliefs to be in the club. God has bigger plans for you and your life.

> For I know the thoughts that I think toward you, says the Lord, thoughts of peace and not of evil, to give you a future and a hope. (Jeremiah 29:11)

Your virtue is something that you would give away. God designed for it to be with your husband. Again, it is given away. It is not taken from you. If it has been taken from you without your consent, that is a violation of God's property. Do not feel that you are any less of a person. You still have just as much value as before. You must see yourself that way. See yourself as having value. If I had a hundred-dollar bill and it had mud all over it, the value of it would still be $100. You need to conduct yourself in a manner of a person that has value. Just because the person is full of lust, it does not give them the right to take anything from you.

> Before I formed you in the womb I knew you, before you were born I set you apart; I appointed you as a prophet to the nations. (Jeremiah 1:5)

You are still precious in God's sight. His love for you has not changed. Mankind will change the love that they have based on performance, situation, and circumstances. When people learn to love you the way that God loves, you will see that type of love will never change. It is like it is in a class all its own.

> Love suffers long and is kind; love does not envy; love does not parade itself, is not puffed up, does not behave rudely, does not seek its own, is not provoked, thinks no evil, does not rejoice in iniquity, but rejoices in the truth; bears all things, believes all things, hopes all things, endures all things. (1 Corinthians 13:4-7)

## WRAP UP

Do not meditate on worry. Meditate on God's Word and His promises. Be slow to respond instead of taking quick actions. You do not want to regret it later. Make the good choice now. Follow God's Word and do not allow your emotions to lead your heart in the decisions that you make. Your heart can change on you. Don't devalue yourself by giving your virtue to anyone that you are not currently married to. Let your worth be determined by who you are in Christ and not by others with wrong intentions.

If there has not been a person that has loved you, look to God. No one can love you the way that He can love in a way that no one else can. I would encourage you to forgive those who have hurt you in the past. It would not be just for them, but also for you. This can help you not to harbor bitterness in the next relationship. It will be pleasing to God.

Line your value with what God says about you. Not by how you may feel or by the wrong things that people may say. Even if you feel less of yourself at times. Even if you have made mistakes. Your value is in what God says about you.

This is a lot that is coming at once. I pray that this is helping, and you can take it in.

## 7
## IMPRESS

Actions are taken to impress someone we are interested in impressing for whatever reason. It can be people that you don't like. It can be those that you are trying to get something from for gain. You may want to be the center of attention. You would like to be the go-to person that everyone would come to for answers. Often times, people will go far out of their way to impress someone that they do not even like. Be sure to ask yourself, "What is the true motive behind what I am doing?" Are you doing the right thing because it is the right thing and you have a large set of eyes on you? If we removed the eyes, would you still do the right thing?

I know that the question was asked before, but what is more important: pleasing God or impressing your friends and others? Do you want to brag about how you have things going for you? Let God put it together as you are being guided by Him. He will do a much better job than we can. He will do a better job of what we call impressing then what we could.

Make sure that you are doing things with the right heart. That will make a lasting impression. This can be seen. These things are normally done anonymously, but God can see your good works and

He knows what is in your heart when you do the things that you do. Good or bad. You do not have to do things to be seen.

> **It is not good to eat much honey; So to seek one's own glory is not glory. (Proverbs 25:27)**

It has always been said, but is so true: "It is not about us." If we can get this instilled in our minds, we would not put so much focus on trying to impress. There would not be as much time spent being worried about what others are thinking. Our time would focus more on what it needs to be focused on.

## IMPRESSING AT THE EXPENSE OF OTHERS

Do not put people down or talk about them as a means of entertainment for others. How would you feel if you were the subject for different jokes for amusement of everyone at the party? Those would be actions that would cause a fight for some. Sadly, this can take place between family members and even a husband and wife. When you do things for the sole purpose of impressing people, you would have to continue doing the same things to keep impressing them. Half the time, the person they are trying to impress, they do not even like. It would not make sense for a husband and wife to put each other down or make them the subjects of jokes to impress people that they do not like. Then they continue with this wrong behavior to attempt to continue to impress people. Not good.

Some want to be the go-to person for their advice and opinions. They want to be praised because of all the so-called knowledge that they give. Sorry to put it this way, but you are not Dr. Phil. I would not encourage you to be Dr. Phil. You will always need to keep this in mind. Only God's counsel will stand the test of time, not our own.

> **There are many plans in a man's heart, Nevertheless the Lord's counsel—that will stand. (Proverbs 19:21)**

We cannot get caught up in ourselves, regardless of how we call ourselves successful with advice and providing our opinions in the past.

Focus on being a better spouse and not impressing people at your spouse's expense. Walk out the things that God has outlined for you in His Word. This would cause the right people to be impressed. You have a light to shine before others in the process of you walking this out. (This would be for both people in the relationship.)

Times will come that you will have to do what is not popular. If you are caught up in impressing people, it will be a harder challenge for you to do what is not popular. Everyone might want to go do the wrong things and go to the wrong places. You will have the have to courage to tell them no. Some people may want to cheat. They may want to lie. Everything they are doing may rest on you going along with it to make it happen. You must have the courage to tell them no. If all the wrong that they are doing rests on you going along with their plan, they must be using you. What I mean by using you is that they need you, and when they are finished, they will no longer have any respect for you. The best thing to do is to start off by having respect for yourself. Stay consistent with God's Word and do it His way.

How are you looking in God's eyes? What is He thinking about you and the actions that you are taking? Don't worry about what the others are thinking. When you put the different things in God's hands, He will be the one that will make your name great. Do not get caught up in the people making your name great. They do not have the control of your name. God will make your name great.

> I will make you a great nation; I will bless you and make your name great; And you shall be a blessing. (Genesis 12:2)

While you are walking things out God's way, He will bless it and cause your name to be great. God will bless the work of your hands because the actions you are taking and the things that you are doing will glorify Him.

## PRIDE

A simple way to look at pride is to say that you overestimate your abilities, talents, resources, and other things that have been afforded to you, while at the same time, you underestimate the same abilities, talents, resources, and things that have been afforded to others. Just because you have not heard the person sing before, it does not mean that the person cannot sing. There are things that you would want to learn about a person or a group before you make any assumptions. It would not be good for you to say you can do something so much better than someone else, only to find out that they can do it so much better than you.

Overpromise and underdeliver. Don't brag or try to one-up next person. This is when someone is competitive in the conversations, emails, text, etc. It is always about them. They dominate the conversation and their opinion is the only one that matters, and they always want the group to do only what they want to do. Everything has to be THEIR WAY.

> **Pride goes before destruction, and a haughty spirit before a fall. (Proverbs 16:18)**

Pride is a dangerous state to be in when you think of your relationships with others. This is an area that we would want to check ourselves. Keep ourselves in check. God's Word tells us that we are to humble ourselves.

> **Humble yourselves in the sight of the Lord, and He will lift you up. (James 4:10)**

The secret is, if you want to go up high, the best thing to do is to get low. It is not the loudest trumpet that gets the attention. Not in God's eyes. Humbling yourself would put you in a position to be lifted. God would lift you up so the right people can see you for the right reasons. Not to say that this will not come without persecution.

> Let another man praise you, and not your own mouth; a stranger, and not your own lips. (Proverbs 27:2)

Do not try to be the center of attention. Earlier it was mentioned to "come out from among them." Have a different way of thinking. You do not have to do what they are doing. They have the lust for the wrong things.

> For they loved the praise of men more than the praise of God. (John 12:43)

God's opinion would be the most important.

> Do not exalt yourself in the presence of the king, And do not stand in the place of the great; For it is better that he say to you, "Come up here," Than that you should be put lower in the presence of the prince, Whom your eyes have seen. (Proverbs 25:6-7)

> As a ring of gold in a swine's snout, So is a lovely woman who lacks discretion. (Proverbs 11:22)

## DEBT

The Jones family cannot be the ones that determine your spending habits. You can be happy for the Jones family and the things that they have; however, you do not have to keep up with them. The Jones family may not have revealed everything that they have done to get all those things that they have. Just because that sister is jumping up and down in the church service to show off her new fur coat does not mean that you must take that credit card and go get one for yourself. It does not mean that you apply pressure to the man to go out and get you a fur coat because you saw someone else with one.

Debt is a topic that is in the other points in this chapter that can be tied in very easily. Impressing at the expense of others, pride, and jealousy are all reasons that could part of why the choice would be made to get into debt. The best defense to counter this attack would be to have the right attitude about the items before you get them. Make sure that you have the things and things do not have you. The different things are not what determine your value. I know the banker and the estate planner will think differently, but this approach will just make you want to get more and more. They make you think more highly of yourself because you have more toys than others. This does not make you any more valuable than the number of friends or likes on social media. Let us put it in perspective. When you are down and out, are those so-called social media "friends" there for you? If you are sick, laying in bed, and need help, what are the likes going to do for you? The true friends will pray for you or come see you.

Live to please God and let all the things that you have glorify Him. Do not live to worship the opinions of others. Let your life glorify God.

There are some things that can be considered that can help you to advance in this area. I will warn you that these are not the popular topics that everyone would want to hear, however they will help to improve. Just as working out and eating the right foods would help the body to be healthy. There are things that can help us become better.

<u>Humbleness</u>. **No, this is not a curse word.** You will not need to get everything that everyone else has now. You do not have to pay the price to impress everyone at the expense of your family or future family. Tomorrow is not promised.

Wait for God to bless you with the right things as you are able to manage them properly, when you can be a good steward over these things. A parent would not want to provide their child with a cell phone until they can see that the child will be responsible. If the child is not responsible, they will not get them the phone. It would not be the right season for them. This parallels with so many other things across the board.

If the child cannot keep up with the phone, they are not ready to have one. If the child is on the phone and not doing their chores or homework, they are not ready for one. If you see the child is so consumed with the phone that they are no longer listening to you or doing the things that you tell them to do, they are not ready to have a phone.

This process would apply for the things that we may been asking God to let us have and we are not ready to handle them properly. We can want God to do things for us and we are not ready to handle the outcome to sustain how He blesses us. This can be in relationships, houses, cars, associations, finances, etc.

<u>Discipline</u>. **No, this is not a curse word.** To some, it may feel like one. This is an area that we all will need to be good stewards. Just like the corporations would delegate the budgets to those that would manage them properly. The people that would do a great job with the budget would save the company money and make them money. They would plan properly for the future of the company and not just think about today. Think about your current family or future family in the same way. Prepare for them. Set the right example for them. Place yourself in a better place that God's blessing can come upon you and your family. Generations that are to come can look to you and your example and see how it is done. They will know that it is possible because they will have seen that it has been done in the past.

> **There is one who makes himself rich, yet has nothing; And one who makes himself poor, yet has great riches. (Proverbs 13:7)**

A quick way to appear like a level of success has been achieved is by getting into debt and getting the things faster. This can dig a bigger hole, causing you to pay more for the item than the original price. It's not a good idea to continue to make payments or interest on a car that you are no longer driving. This is stealing from a future that this money could be building.

This reminds me about someone making a visit to a car dealership and viewing all the new cars that are on the car lot. The person could be making a routine trip to have their car serviced for the car that they are driving currently. They walk out to the car lot to see the inventory. They can see the different models along with any new releases for any different models that are coming out soon. The same model is on the floor that they are getting serviced; however, it is a younger model.

The salesperson convinces them to take a test drive. The person gets in and begins to see everything new. New leather. New look. Even has the new car smell. They take the test drive and the car rides so smooth. That should not be a surprise because it is a new car. Everything is clean and the car is shining. The tires have the shiny gloss as others can see the shiny rims going round and round. Heads turn as they ride around the block so they can see it at the stop light.

Time comes to an end and they return the car to the dealership while the salesperson is still in the car riding along. As they come into the parking lot, the new car is strategically parked right beside the person's old car that just got serviced. The psychology behind this is that the person must leave all the newness to get back into that old car that they drove to the dealership. That is not by accident. Do not fall into the debt trap. When the newness wears off, the monthly bill is still in place.

What I find to be interesting is that as soon as the person gets back in the old car, they start to complain. The radio is not good enough. It does not ride as smooth as the new car. They notice dents in the car that were there all along. Seems like everything with the old car is now such a big issue. Now **sooo** much seems to be wrong with the old car that the person drove to the dealership.

Nothing was wrong with the car when they drove it to the dealership. There was no problem with the radio while driving to the dealership. The car drove fine without an issue. The person was getting it serviced as it should be serviced. The dents in the car were not noticed. There was not one issue with the car as the person drove to be serviced.

The true issue is that the person is desiring a new car. They are no longer appreciating the car that they have currently. Someone could have made a big sacrifice for the old car that you're driving. You will get to that new car quicker by being thankful for the one that you have and continuing to take care of it and being a good steward over the car. It is getting things off to a good start by getting the car serviced.

There is a parable of the talents that is found in the book of Matthew in the Bible. It talks about a man traveling to a far country. The man gave talents to his servants according to their ability. He gave one servant five talents, he gave two to another servant, and one talent to another. The servant that had five gained five more. The servant that was given two gained another two talents. The servant that was with one talent did not trade to gain as the other two were able to do. The servant with one talent was afraid and hid the talent that was given to him in the ground. That did not profit anyone. The response may have seemed harsh, but talent was placed in the hands of someone that would manage it better.

> **But his lord answered and said to him, "You wicked and lazy servant, you knew that I reap where I have not sown, and gather where I have not scattered seed. So you ought to have deposited my money with the bankers, and at my coming I would have received back my own with interest. So take the talent from him, and give it to him who has ten talents." (Matthew 25:26-28)**

Part of being thankful is taking care of what has been given to you. This includes being a good steward. Being a bad steward would cause items to be taken away. When the car is not maintained properly, it could break down to the point that it cannot be repaired or to a point that it would be too expensive to repair. Hence, the car is taken away.

The good steward would take care of the car and have maintenance done to the car on a regular basis. When the time comes that a new or newer car is considered, the car can be sold for a higher price. 1. There is still a car, 2. It can be sold for a higher price, 3. There is more money to go toward a new or newer car. The good steward would be in a better position to move forward. I just wanted to provide this as an example to explain how this parable could apply to you.

An old car can be sold for a higher amount than what it was purchased brand new. This may be hard to believe, that this can be done without taking advantage of someone, but it can. It would depend on the steward of the car. As the car ages and it can be seen that car has the original paint and other original items in great condition, the car will hold value. The car can be placed in different auto shows. There can also be in demand for different film productions because the make and model of that car is needed for the film. The value of the car can go up more because this actor was in a scene with this car in a film. All because the right steward had the car.

It has been said all so often, the number of miles that are on the car does not matter. If you have a decent car, the main concern would be is to know that the car was taken care of by the previous owner or owners. If the car was taken care of, it will last. We can think about this same process and how it can apply to the different things in our life: a house, relationships, career, family, community, etc. Think outside of the box on maintaining and taking care of this as an example of the good steward with the car.

You may not have the expensive car and the big house to start. Practice living within your means. Learn to operate with the resources that you have. This can allow the extra that comes in to be extra. This can stop you from robbing Peter to pay Paul. You do not need the exterior things to impress, to try to make your stock more valuable. Again, let God make your name great. No need to go into debt for the things. The things do not validate your worth. If you invited Christ in your life, you are God's child. If you can get into His Word, you can get a better understanding of the value that you hold.

> Beloved, now we are children of God; and it has not yet been revealed what we shall be, but we know that when He is revealed, we shall be like Him, for we shall see Him as He is. (1 John 3:2)

Do not despise the day of small beginnings. Be grateful where you are and believe God for your increase.

## SMALL BEGINNINGS

> For who has despised the day of small things? For these seven rejoice to see The plumb line in the hand of Zerubbabel. They are the eyes of the Lord, Which scan to and fro throughout the whole earth. (Zechariah 4:10)

## INCREASE

> He will bless those who fear the Lord, Both small and great. May the Lord give you increase more and more, You and your children. (Psalm 115:13-14)

Think of driving down a highway and someone comes behind you and begins to tailgate you to get you to move or drive faster. Do not let this person's actions determine your response. They do not control what you are to do next. You set the pace. (The speed limit would be a good start.) You do not have to run in the rat race or be driven by someone else by getting into debt to keep up, nor do anything else for that matter.

## JEALOUSY

Another reason that debt would occur would be that there is jealousy against someone else. A person can see all that someone else may have and feel that they do not deserve all that they have and try to get the same for themselves. Life is not a contest to see who can get the most toys.

You would want to be happy for others and their achievements. This is a way that we can be thankful and trust and believe that ours is on the way. God's Word tells us that we are to rejoice with them.

> Rejoice with those who rejoice, and weep with those who weep. (Romans 12:15)

When someone gets a new house, congratulate them. When a they get a promotion on the job, congratulate them. If they get engaged, congratulate them. When a child is born, congratulate them. When they have an anniversary, congratulate them.

When you congratulate them, you are sowing a good seed. You are showing God that you are believing that yours is on the way. I know you will not like to hear what I am about to say, but I am going to say it anyway. This may be a good time to sow a seed into the person's life. Help break that jealousy.

**Give**. This is not a curse word. I know you may not want to do this at this time. I can help you get the wrong feelings out of your heart. Besides, it will be a choice, not a feeling. Rejoicing would be a choice and not a feeling.

> Wrath is cruel and anger a torrent, But who is able to stand before jealousy? (Proverbs 27:4)

If a person is angry, they are angry, but jealousy can be more dangerous than being angry. You will want to have a heart check and be sure that your heart is in the right place. The first murder in the Bible was because of jealousy.

If the person has a new car, you can give them a gift card for gas. If they just purchased a home, you could provide a housewarming gift. If the person is getting married, you can provide a gift that would be something that would help keep their marriage strong. Maybe a book on marriage. Whatsoever a man sows that will he reap, so you will want to use this time to sow a good seed. This would be a help to you to get what you are seeking: the right things. You are working to get your heart right.

> "Be angry, and do not sin": do not let the sun go down on your wrath. (Ephesians 4:26)

Something else that we can do to stay out of jealousy is to mind our own business. This might be a challenge for some, but this can be done. Minding your own business will keep you focused on your business. This would be part of removing the distractions.

A good example of this would be in the workplace. Sister Susie was doing good and everything was going well. She had a great attitude and was a pleasant person to work with while being in the office. Everyone got along with Sister Susie and loved to be around her at work.

One day, Sister Susie finds out that someone who was just hired is making more money. Now Sister Susie is quiet at work. She is not as sociable as she once was in the past. She is not friendly because she is upset. It does not matter about how Sister Susie got the information. The fact that her entire demeaner has changed is making matters worse for her. If she would have minded her own business, this would not have occurred. She would have continued to be the nice person everyone wanted to work beside.

She does not know that she could be in line for a raise or a promotion. The company or organization might have needed to hire someone to be in place before they promoted Sister Susie. The person may have more qualifications and may be given more responsibilities than Sister Susie. Now that Sister Susie has found out a new person is being paid more than she is being paid, she has an attitude. Everyone can tell. What if all the plans for Sister Susie were stopped because of her attitude? **Mind your own business.** This can stop you from hindering what God has for you. Continue to trust God to be your source.

## WHAT ARE YOU ATTRACTING?

People can go to great lengths to try to impress someone. Someone can go to the gym and workout hard and starve themselves to get the figure of the woman in the magazine. If that is what is going to attract the person, what happens if there is a weight gain? Will the attraction go away with the weight gain? Again, what you do to impress, or shall we say to attract them, you will have to continue to do to keep them around. It would be a lot easier on you if you would just be yourself.

It is funny how the single woman would get her hair done every week. She's always shopping and having a nice outfit on hand. New shoes all the time. In the gym working out almost every day. Makes herself familiar with the trends. Makes sure she is aware of everything that the men are interested in, such as football, basketball, cars, and other things. When she gets involved with him, all those things stop and she wonders why he is not coming home at night. I'm not saying that this is acceptable. This does not give the man an excuse to no longer be attracted to you. I just wanted you to look at all the work that went in to impressing him. If it took those things to get his interest, we would not want to take things for granted. Make sure you are doing things with the right motive. If you could watch the game with him to get involved with him, do not stop after you get in a relationship with the person. Sister, let us do things God's way. Let God lead you to the right person where your common interest will come naturally, not something that you tried to make happen. Be yourself. Be the person God created you to be.

I have two cousins that had luxury cars back when I was just out of high school. One of them asked me to drive his car while he was adjusting his sound system. As we approached the light, people started to pop up out of the blue. Started seeing cars full of girls drive up and speaking, trying to get our attention. My cousin began to say to me, "Don't pay them any attention. It is just the car. It's not about the people in the car. They are just looking at the car. Don't pay them any attention." We have another cousin that is older than us. He has a car that was even more expensive. At the time, he was living in a bigger city and he had the same experience. When talking to him, he told us that he took the advice from those that have the same kind of car that he drives: "Put your windows all the way up. Smile, wave, and keep on driving. That will keep everybody out of trouble." Sounds like it was a common thing for people where he was living at the time.

Everything plays a part. Look at the things you have and what they are attracting. Everything from the clothes that you wear, the car you drive, the people that you hang around, and the places that you go. They will all attract a certain element to you, good or bad.

As much as I would hate to have to bring this up, it must be said. You must monitor what you are wearing. There is a totally different dynamic from the way a man would look and think about a woman by the way she is dressed compared to how a woman may see how a man is dressed. A man will look and think about a woman in a business suit differently compared to woman wearing something that is very tight and that is revealing her body.

In general, he would look at one person for something long term and not look at the other person in the same light. Men are turned on by sight; however, a gentleman would look for something long term. He would want a lady that he could bring home to introduce to the family. As a Christian, there would not be any sexual activity until after marriage.

The bad boy would look for a temporary fling. They want to keep everything quiet and not want anyone to know. They may have to do things in a way that others would not know. He will pressure you from time to time. Keep in mind that if you must participate in the different things that he pressures you to do, you will have to continue to do them to keep his interest.

Do not let what you are wearing attract the wrong person or send the wrong message. Consistently wearing the wrong thing can attract the wrong person, which in turn can put you in a situation that you may not be able to handle. I'm not saying that you dressing inappropriately would give anyone the right to treat you badly. What I am saying is not give them a place or a thought for them to even look at you in the wrong way.

- Boys: Players play
- Men: Plan
- Boys: Have swag (to impress)
- Men: Have class (it can be seen)
- Boys: Keep saying they are going to do something one day

- Men: Decree a thing and apply their faith until it is manifested
- Boys: Do what they can (do what they can get away with doing)
- Men: Walk out desires God placed in their heart

## WRAP UP

You do not have to impress. The gift that God has given you will make room for you. God will see you are noticed by the right person. Focus on your gifts, talents, and abilities. The room will be set for whatever you're seeking it to be: a marriage, job, business, album, book, acting role, or whatever it is that you desire. Let God bring you the divine connection. No need to perform works to force something.

Spend your time developing yourself to be the good steward over what you are believing for God to do for you. This will show God you are serious about being a good steward over what He blesses you with and how you will honor Him with what He does for you.

# 8
## DON'T COME AGAINST HIM

When looking through history, we can see there were many great men that have achieved many great things. Even looking at all the accomplishments, a good woman can be seen by their side. The saying has been said time and time again: behind every good man is a good woman. That can be a wife, mother, grandmother, teacher, etc.

The right woman would be a tremendous value to the man. There are countless conversations that kings would have with their queens that have taken place that we are unaware. There are men who can rule countries, businessmen run corporations, men in high positions with great responsibilities all making decisions. They want to be sure that they have considered every aspect. They will want to get it from someone that they can trust, that does not have a wrong motive. This is just an example of how priceless that right woman can be.

> Who can find a virtuous wife? For her worth is far above rubies. (Proverbs 31:10)

I have seen this myself personally. A man would have a vision. It would be something that he is passionate about doing. When that right woman is there, it is like a gift that she has from God to put the fine details in place that would make it work. When working in projects in the corporate world, it is amazing how some women can get the details together that others would overlook. It is not a threat to them, but she is trying to help and work along with them by adding value.

The example that I always think about is when man brings up a trip to say, "Let's spend the weekend over here or there with the family." The woman begins to ask questions. Where will we stay? What will we eat? How long will we be there? The man has not thought all of this through at this point. He is just thinking about a trip and contemplating where to go. When the major decisions have been made, it would only be a matter of time before the lady's gift kicks in and she would share the information on the options that are available.

> And the Lord God said, "It is not good that man should be alone; I will make him a helper comparable to him." (Genesis 2:18)

Being that right woman with the man's best interest at heart would have the woman to be an asset to the man. Being the wrong woman would do more harm than good. Being the helpmate would cause more to be accomplished by the two working together. Staying together, being focused on the goals, and building each other up will help remove the distractions.

Don't worry about where he is or what he is doing. You are right there working with them. People cannot poison your mind with negative images because you will know the truth. It is a lot easier to cast down imaginations when you know the truth. You were with him the entire time.

## STOP TRYING TO CHANGE HIM

Too many people fall into the mindset that they can change someone. They meet the person and begin to size them up to force a fit. The things that they see are overlooked because they feel that they will get that changed later down the road. They try to force this relationship to fit when it does not. This is like having an outfit where someone is trying to force the colors together in an attempt to make the colors in the outfit match. It is clear that they need to put on something else. They get their feelings involved and find out the hard way that this person cannot be changed. They get upset and go on the emotional roller coaster and never seem to get off. God is the only one that can profoundly change a person. Other than that, people can fool you for a season. They can allow you to think a certain way about who they are, or make you think they have changed long enough to get whatever it is that they want. Allow the person to be who they are, then evaluate the fruit and see if this is who God would have you to move forward with in a relationship. Do not pressure them into being what you want them to be by comparing the relationship to others, social media, magazines, and other outside influences.

When you take control by applying the wrong pressure, you limit God's ability to create in man what God wants him to be. You would not allow God to do the exceedingly, abundantly, above all you can ask or think. You are trying to conform him to what you are seeing around you. Imagine God changing him to a person that is so good for you that you have not even been exposed to him yet.

> **Now to Him who is able to do exceedingly abundantly above all that we ask or think, according to the power that works in us... (Ephesians 3:20)**

Let God put it together. Let Him pick the person for you. Let Him get you prepared. Let Him work on the changes that are to take place. You will appreciate it more when it is coming from Him. You will be a better steward over things that you know came from God.

If your thoughts are constantly negative, you are not giving God anything to work with on making a change. If you are always making negative comments about the man, you are not giving God a lot to work with on making a change in the man. I would encourage you to allow the man to be who God has created him to be. Many of the things about him could be part of the destiny that God has for him to complete. There may be things that you like or may dislike that you see in the man. You want to be careful that the things that you are trying to change are for the right reasons. You want to be sure that they do not disrupt what God's plan for the person's life would be. You can provide what I would call a positive push in the right direction. The right type of encouragement. In providing the right encouragement, you can enhance what is already there inside the person. This can be something that you can seek God to help you with.

I was reading a book written by Diana Hagee called *What Every Woman Wants in A Man*. She is the wife to the pastor John Hagee. In the book, she told a story about how she had a prayed about how she wanted God to change her husband. She had a prayer list that she prayed day after day for the changes to take place in her husband. She finally got an answer to her prayer.

God was going to deliver her the husband that she had been praying to have. The changes from the list that she had were going to be made. She was excited to be getting this from God. Then she began to get the rest of the message: God was going to make the changes for her; however, God will no longer be able to use her husband.

The Holy Spirt begin to give her the revelation that the traits that God put in her husband were the ones that He placed in him to use for His purpose. He can deliver the message in a way that he can be effective. As a result of this, lives of people have been changed.

I have a great deal of respect for this because she was more interested in him being in the center of God's will. All the other things no longer mattered. She made God priority above what people thought. Even above what she thought. It would be a blessing to have more women like her that would seek God. They seek God's opinion above their own.

> Charm is deceitful and beauty is passing, But a woman who fears the Lord, she shall be praised. (Proverbs 31:30)

## LET GOD DEVELOP HIM FOR HIS AGENDA

Tearing a person down to build them up, programing them differently into what you want them to be is not a process that I would recommend. The process that many would use is to tear the person down and have them to feel as if they are worthless and that they cannot do anything right. Have them feel that everyone would be displeased with the person unless they accomplish certain things. When they get the person to the lowest point, they begin to build the person up by programing the person to be what they would want the person to be. This process has taken place in the past in many situations. Some people are not even aware that they are taking this approach with someone because it has become so common place.

I am going to call this what it is: WITCHCRAFT. I know when this term is used, the thoughts would come of a group of people giving a chant or casting spells. This still has the same traits. Someone is trying to control someone else to cause them to do what they want the person to do. This can be seen in different organizations, the place of work, and so many other places as you can imagine. Do not do this to anyone.

> An excellent wife is the crown of her husband, But she who causes shame is like rottenness in his bones. (Proverbs 12:4)

I would encourage you to work with him as he is following God. As mentioned earlier, God's Word said that He will make him a helper comparable to him. Be that helper that he needs. I know some are saying he is not following God or anything about God. You can win him over by the change that he can see in you. This will not work if he sees you doing the wrong things and participate in all those things with him. When he can see you change, it opens the door for him to change. I have seen it happen in my own family. I encourage you to be the crown and not the rottenness in his bones. Look for ways to work with him and not against him.

> Wives, likewise, be submissive to your own husbands, that even if some do not obey the word, they, without a word, may be won by the conduct of their wives, when they observe your chaste conduct accompanied by fear. Do not let your adornment be merely outward—arranging the hair, wearing gold, or putting on fine apparel rather let it be the hidden person of the heart, with the incorruptible beauty of a gentle and quiet spirit, which is very precious in the sight of God. For in this manner, in former times, the holy women who trusted in God also adorned themselves, being submissive to their own husbands... (1 Peter 3:1-5)

As the change would take place in your life for God, you can then let God use him for His purpose as it pleases Him. The gifts, talents, and abilities can be developed for God's kingdom to allow God to get the glory. This would be as a person would receive a special gift and they would cherish the gift so much that they would develop it and take care of it to the point that they would give it back in a greater condition than what was given to them. A Scripture comes to mind when I think on this:

> The twenty-four elders fall down before Him who sits on the throne and worship Him who lives forever and ever, and cast their crowns before the throne, saying: "You are worthy, O Lord, To receive glory and honor and power; For You created all things, And by Your will they exist and were created." (Revelation 4:10-11)

I would look at the crowns as the gift that was given to them, but they cast it down before the throne as a gift to the one that created them to use the gift that He gave to them.

## ATTACKING WITHOUT GETTING THE TRUTH

People can come up to you and tell you anything. I mentioned how dangerous jealousy can be in one of the earlier chapters. Consider the source. Get an understanding as to why this person is telling you the different things that they are telling you. If it is truly out of love and someone is trying to prevent you from being hurt, that would be one thing to consider. On the other hand, you can have someone that does not know you that well and they do not have a vested interest in your life. They can tell you anything to get a reaction out of you. They may want to cause issues in your home just to get things going. Be careful about who you are sharing your life details. A jealous person may not want to see you happy. As it has been said, hurt people hurt people. Do not go off on a tangent and harm other people on a whim or off-the-cuff comment. The enemy comes to steal, kill, and destroy. Do not give the enemy any place in your life.

> **The simple believes every word, but the prudent considers well his steps. (Proverbs 14:15)**

If you find yourself believing every word, take the time to believe God's. Put the pressure and the trust on His Word and not the person. Think about God's promises. Open the Bible and look over those promises and speak them out again and again. Get the truth about the situation and get the truth in God's Word. Regardless how things may look around you, God's Word will not come back void.

The words and advice from others will often come back void. People can have a misunderstanding. They can see things differently. The outcome of the things seen or talked about can be totally wrong. You are not able to always take things at face value. When you attack someone with the wrong information, you can do some serious damage. It has been said not to burn your bridges. Actions like this may not burn the bridge, but some damage can be beyond repair. The bridge can still be in place, but not be able to handle all the weight that it was able to carry in the past.

There may have been conversations that took place in the past freely before the person was attacked. Now they may be more closed off than before. It can be a challenge with trust after being attacked and falsely accused. They are not sure if anything they do will be misunderstood or taken the wrong way. They aren't sure if their words will be turned around and used against them. The person will be guarded and cautious moving forward. It may take some time for this bridge to have some repairs; however, things may not go back to the way they were.

## DON'T POKE HOLES IN YOUR COVERING

The man is supposed to be the head of the home. By being the head of the home, he would need to cover the home in prayer. It may not seem as the big macho thing that is portrayed on television; however, it has more impact. The prayer of the righteous do avail much. There was only one person that I remember that prayed out openly with no problem. I was goofing off with my friends at their home. I stepped back and tripped over their father. I said I was sorry. Then I found that the reason that he was kneeling was because he was praying. I felt even worse when I found this out. I was in the kitchen playing and this man was in the living room praying. More of us men need to take our place in prayer. Their dad was not ashamed. When you have someone that is making efforts to do this, do not be a challenge to him doing this for the home, family, business, or whatever the need for prayer.

> **Better to dwell in a corner of a housetop, than in a house shared with a contentious woman. (Proverbs 21:9)**

By being a challenge, I am speaking about you not being the contentious woman to this man. Don't be the argumentative, quarrelsome, debatable person. The one who always has to be right about everything. It's better for him to be on the roof top. What gets me is when a person continues to speak negatively about their husband, time and time again. I am thinking you do not realize this man may be the covering for you in prayer. Why do all these negative things against the husband? I certainly hope you are not doing this to your pastor or those in leadership that are praying for you. If the man is on the roof top dealing with the elements of the weather, how can he be in prayer covering you? How effective can this man be praying for you, dealing with the different things of great magnitude, only to be distracted by something that is not important?

I know there are times that things are done that make you upset. Don't look to hurt him by doing and saying things in the dark, thinking you can come against him without him knowing. God sees everything. Keep yourself free of any negative activity toward the man.

> For there is nothing covered that will not be revealed, nor hidden that will not be known. Therefore whatever you have spoken in the dark will be heard in the light, and what you have spoken in the ear in inner rooms will be proclaimed on the housetops. (Luke 12:2-3)

Let good things be spoken about you. Not the wrong things, but the good things. Continue to work with him and not against him.

## I NEED TO TEACH HIM A LESSON

If you find yourself making this statement or even having this thought, you have clearly not forgiven. This thought process is already starting off as if a wrong decision is about to be made. This will affect you in more ways than just one. Whatsoever a man sows that he will also reap. It would be a good practice to reap good things and have the good things to come back to you.

> Do not be deceived: God cannot be mocked. A man reaps what he sows. Whoever sows to please their flesh, from the flesh will reap

destruction; whoever sows to please the Spirit, from the Spirit will reap eternal life. (Galatians 6:7-8)

To avoid making the wrong decision, you would want to start off with forgiving. Jesus mentioned this in God's Word. Forgiving would be an act of showing love. We do not have to wait for the person to ask for forgiveness. You may not want to hear this, but in many cases, the person will not ask for forgiveness or say, "I am sorry." We can forgive anyway.

> **And when you stand praying, if you hold anything against anyone, forgive them, so that your Father in heaven may forgive you your sins. (Mark 11:25)**

You are sowing a bad seed by trying to teach a lesson. Getting to the heart of the matter, it is truly revenge. Whatever you do, you will not be able to take it back. Be slow to speak. Slow to wrath. Slow to approach. Make sure you have all the information, not just what you think that you know. You will want to reap from a good seed, not a bad one.

> **Rejoice not when your enemy falls, and let not your heart be glad when he stumbles or is overthrown, Lest the Lord see it and it be evil in His eyes and displease Him, and He turn away His wrath from him [to expend it upon you, the worse offender]. (Proverbs 24:17-18 \*Amplified Bible, Classic Edition)**

Be careful with those comments to state, "They got what they deserved" or "That is what they get." Forgive. You may not feel like it, but remember that it is a choice, not a feeling. Many of us have learned from a child that when we are hit, we're supposed to hit the person back. We're supposed to go to great lengths to get the person back and make them pay for what they did. God's Word gives us instructions on handling this situation.

Beloved, do not avenge yourselves, but rather give place to wrath; for it is written, "Vengeance is Mine, I will repay," says the Lord. (Romans 12:19)

"Vengeance is Mine," says the Lord. It is not yours to take. Not physically, not in a court room, not with gossip, not by trying to make him look bad. Not by turning his child against him by bad mouthing him. Not by trying to turn family and friends against him. Not by playing the victim on every topic. The vengeance is the Lord's. Not yours. This is with all things being in general. If there is danger such as violence, rape, domestic abuse, or your child being abused, you are to get yourself and your children to safety.

Others are seeing what is taking place. People are watching. I remember being in my old neighborhood as a teenager. There was a couple that fought (argued) every Friday night. It was like clockwork. At the same time every Friday, they would be arguing with each other. I was outside in the parking lot talking to one of my friends and we all could hear them going at it in the apartment where they were living. My friend said they do this every Friday night. I thought he was kidding. The times that I would be around there on a Friday night, I found what he said to be true. You could set your clock and ring a bell to this couple getting started. They would be so loud, everyone in the parking lot would be able to hear the couple. Like this was a drama sitcom that came on Fridays that people could watch for entertainment. "Let's see what is going to happen this week."

You may not believe it, but there are others that are watching you. They are looking at the actions that are being taken and how this is being addressed. I'm not saying that you will be as obvious or loud as the couple that I mentioned; however, some people are watching you. Some may follow your lead and do the same thing in their relationships. Others may choose not to follow. As a Christian, you are to set the example. If you have children that are in your life, it will be critical how you handle things. You are the living, breathing example that they will think about when they come across a similar situation.

When you handle things in a godly manner, you are not only putting yourself in a position for God to bless you, but you are letting your light shine to others. It may look a little weak at first compared to others, but do it God's way. This would be part of humbling yourself, as we mentioned before. I'm not saying to let someone take advantage of you. Doing it God's way would let Him intervene and provide you with better results in the long run. You must mix your faith with your actions as you are taking steps according to God's Word.

## MAKE SURE YOU ARE COMPLETE

When I say to make sure that you are complete, it is to be sure that you are complete in Christ. Not in anything else. Be confident in who you are and what God is creating you to be.

> For we are His workmanship, created in Christ Jesus for good works, which God prepared beforehand that we should walk in them. (Ephesians 2:10)

Many are battling with insecurities. Do not look to social status or anything else to determine your value. The likes on social media do not make you the success that God desires for you, the light that He would want you to be for others.

Make sure you are with a godly man and not a bad boy. The bad boy will have you on an emotional roller coaster going around in circles again and again. The reason being is because the bad boy would take advantage of the situation and use it to his advantage. The godly man would look to see how the need can be met in your life. He would need to seek God on his approach to minister to your needs in this area. This is not to put this all on one person. If you are having challenges and you are fighting insecurities, you have a part to play. Being honest about it would be good start. Not playing the blame game. Being honest and taking steps to address the issue is more honorable than being in denial. Work to address it at the root.

If this is the person that God gave you, hold on and focus on the word that God gave you pertaining this man. We spoke earlier in this letter about spending time with God and communicating with Him in prayer. You would need to have peace about the type of person and the relationship prior to getting involved. If you missed it or if you moved too fast, there is no shame in admitting that you made a mistake. If you find that you made the mistake yourself, a mistake that has caused a problem in the relationship, go ahead and admit it and make it right. Do not remain in pride or play the victim and blame anyone and everyone else. Change what you can change within yourself.

## WRAP UP

Many might shy away from relationships because they can seem to be more of a distraction than something fruitful. It would be more productive to move forward in what God has set someone out to do than to be held back by things that are trivial. Having a helpmate would mean this would be someone that would be a help to cross the finish line faster. There are enough attacks against the person that is trying to do the right thing. It is not good for them to get with someone that adds to the attacks that are already occurring. The helpmate would be the asset by standing beside them in the fight. As society and different groups would attack the man of God, he would have the right helpmate that would operate in line with God's Word. Do not let society or culture change what God's Word says.

# 9
# DIFFERENT CULTURES

With all the different cultures that cover the world, I am sure there are some that we are not aware of. There are so many that they all could not be named. Some cultures will do things out of tradition and others may do things because of their beliefs.

When thinking about the different cultures, there would be thoughts that come to mind just by them being mentioned. There would be a perception that a person would have in mind by the mention of the culture alone.

- Mormons
- Amish
- Muslims
- Indians
- Chinese
- Lebanese
- African
- Canadian
- Latino
- Japanese

What are all the good traits that come to mind? Are you thinking about work ethic, supportiveness, or loyalty? I know that we may not know about every culture, but what are some of the good things that come to mind? I'm not saying anything against the religions or cultures. Can we have God exalted above all?

When we think about a Christian, what comes to mind? Would the character outweigh the thoughts on how the Christian culture is being perceived? I wanted to put a perspective on who is being represented. **Christ.** We would want to have the best representation of **Christ** in anything and everything that is done: in relationships with others, how we work, how we treat people, etc. When it comes to a Christian, there should be positive things that comes to everyone's mind. Even if we are hated, we should be hated for the right reason.

> If the world hates you, keep in mind that it hated me first. (John 15:18)

**Virgin** is not a dirty word. If you are rejected because you are a virgin, do not feel down. Stand firm on what you believe. Keep living the life of Christ and do not compromise who you are in Him. Regardless of what others may say about you. They cannot get back what they gave away. Hold on to your virtue.

With the actions that are taken, we must represent Christ well. God has love for everyone. He is not a man that could lie. Even if others are not following Christ, God still loves them.

> ...that you may be sons of your Father in heaven; for He makes His sun rise on the evil and on the good, and sends rain on the just and on the unjust. (Matthew 5:45)

If we meet the conditions by being obedient to God, He will bless the fruit of our ground.

> Blessed shall be the fruit of your body, the produce of your

ground and the increase of your herds, the increase of your cattle and the offspring of your flocks. (Deuteronomy 28:4)

We may have the same amount of sunshine and the same amount of rain. The difference would be that God would bless what we have done. We can expect God to bless the work of our hands. We may see that others are getting ahead and that the nice guy is finishing last. When you are doing it God's way, you will not lose.

You will find that the seeds that were planted grow more and more and bigger than the normal. You can say that God put His "super" on our "natural." We would have a surplus on what we were expecting because of the blessing of the Lord.

As it was stated in the Scripture, God makes the sun to rise on the evil and the good. He sends rain on the just and the unjust. So even when others operate in the principles, they still get some return. The return is not as blessed as the believer's return, but it still yields a return. You can notice that when the corporations give how it comes back to them. When people who are not Christians give, they get a return on their giving and they encourage others to do the same.

When you see others practice the principles, you can see they reap the benefits. Some of the things that they practice are part of their family's tradition or some of the things that they do are part of the culture. They may have never made it to a church for anyone to tell them the principle. They may have grown up doing the things that they were taught.

This is not a reason to get upset or jealous of anyone. We wonder how others are getting better results in different areas. The first thing that we must check is to see that we meet the qualifications for the blessing of God to be on us. Are we being obedient? Are we practicing our love walk? Are we staying consistent with God's Word?

If a culture has a 5% divorce rate and we have 50%, it does not mean to get mad at anyone. Nothing against anyone else. We can look in the mirror and see how we can do better. How can we be a better witness for Christ? What would need to be done to step up our game? Are we doing all that we can to be pleasing in God's sight?

By looking at people, we can see that they come from strong cultures with a long history. The different things in their culture have been passed down from generation to generation. The cultures are so strong that they did not allow anything to distract or influence the long history that their rich culture provides. Honesty, integrity, discipline, loyalty, and others are a few of the things that are part of many cultures. These values are all part of the package. As the traditions and culture are passed down, they do not change. I wish I could say it would remain the same for everyone. If we can work to be more like Jesus Christ, we would have consistency in this regard. He was very consistent. God's Word makes a reference to this consistency.

**Jesus Christ is the same yesterday, today, and forever. (Hebrews 13:8)**

No outside influences would cause Him to change His mind about anything. Could you image Jesus going to the cross one minute and then stopping and saying He is going to do something else because this was not popular or He was worried about what people would think? If Jesus would have been that easy to stop or change, the devil would not have had to put a lot of work in coming against Jesus. Jesus stayed true to who He was and what He was called to be.

I think about someone that only met his biological father once in his life and he was only a baby at the time. He grew up with a fascination for cars that he was not able to explain. It could be seen that there was something unique about the person. His fascination has driven him to taking auto mechanic classes during his high school years. There were some challenges with the teacher; however, he still finished the classes in high school. After high school, he began to work in the industry and started to see what was needed to pursue a career in the field. He took some courses and got his certifications and he was able to get a job working on cars. This was what he loved. You may be saying, "What does that have to do with anything?" Well, years later, this man was reconnected with his biological family.

When he reconnected, he found that all of his uncles were

mechanics. He knew that his biological father was a mechanic. I find it interesting that even being raised in an environment outside of his biological family, he picked up so many of the traditions from his biological family while being separated. He became a part of what the family was known for being and accomplished what they would have expected. Some things were passed down that were not literally passed down, in a matter of speaking.

If we can continue in the things of God, we can stay consistent with what His Word states. This would help us to keep a renewed mind and not sell ourselves short and be men pleasers. By continuing in His Word and continuing to go to church, it can help us to be consistent with God and do the things that Jesus did. It is in the blood.

Regardless of the attacks against the marriage that God designed, even if there is an agenda against the foundation of the home, even when society attacks the man... you remain the same. Staying with God's Word does not mean that this is hate. You are choosing to stay with God. God's Word tells us to do good to all. God's Word tells us to even love our enemies.

> Therefore, as we have opportunity, let us do good to all, especially to those who are of the household of faith. (Galatians 6:10)

> You have heard that it was said, "You shall love your neighbor and hate your enemy." But I say to you, love your enemies, bless those who curse you, do good to those who hate you, and pray for those who spitefully use you and persecute you... (Matthew 5:43-44)

Yes, we still love those that are attacking God's foundation. Still we are to pray for them, even though if they do not want to change and continue to go against the things that God has designed.

## DATE JESUS

This may sound strange, but hear me out. If you have challenges in your relationships with people and you are currently a Christian, I encourage you to date Jesus. I heard this term used and found it to be a little odd when I first heard this mentioned. When you spend time with someone, you learn more about them than what you knew before. The time that would normally be spent doing other things can be spent in God's Word, getting in God's presence, and being in prayer with God. It was mentioned in the earlier chapter that I never sought out to do this on my own; however, due to circumstances, I found myself being around the things of God more and more.

If your time is spent going out on the weekends and being consumed with other activities, you are missing out. Taking this time out will help you to manage all the other things that you are doing. It will help you in your approach in the relationships that you have: on the job, in the home, or in other relationships that you would be interested in having in the future.

I personally found that things would just come to me, like how to handle this situation or that situation. Answers would flow and I would know what to do. It may not have been the most popular thing at the time, but it helped me out in the long term. Making the right decisions and keeping the boundaries up where they needed to be caused this to be a big difference in my life. Taking the time to do this helped more than I can explain.

If there is something that you find a struggle with defeating, replace the time that you would spend doing those things with spending time with God. If you are going places that you know you should not be going, replace the time by spending time with God. You will find a desire to spend more time doing the right things instead of the wrong things.

## MY DREAM

It would be great if we got back to the things are in God's Word. Being the village that has the environment that the children could be raised. Being that trusted responsible village that God could entrust the children to live in and be a part of the community.

I remember the older generations speaking about how their parents were not the only ones that whipped them if they did something wrong. The neighbors and others that knew your parents would whip them as if they were their own children. They would be quick to discipline them whenever they were out of line. When everyone was done correcting them, their parents got the final round when they walked in the house. By the time they got home, the parents knew what happened and they would be ready to discipline. The word would have reached the parents by that time.

I am so glad that I did not have to live through that time frame; however, I did feel a sense of family in the neighborhood. I did not get a whipping by everyone in the neighborhood as the previous generation did. The parents of the other children would speak to me and correct me as if I were one of their own. They did not put any hands on me, but they showed love by correcting me when needed. Encouraging wherever needed. There was a sense of community as if we are all in this together. As the families would be able to move out of the apartment to a house, the support would always be there for one another as we crossed one another's path. You don't forget where you came from. Remember those that were with you while you were there.

There was a candy lady in our neighborhood. This would be a place to go to purchase candy, snacks, sodas, and other things of this nature. The space behind her cash register was one huge wallpaper collage of pictures of everyone in our neighborhood and the neighborhood behind ours. It was like a wall of fame that included you because your picture would be on the wall. All types of pictures would be on the wall: school pictures, prom pictures, wedding pictures, newborn baby pictures. When I graduated from high school, her grandson came to me and gave me a congratulations card with a stuffed animal from the candy lady. I was thankful for the gift and, as you may already know, my graduation picture was on the wall. That wall was a connection to us all. This was a small part of being the village. I would like to get back to that once again.

I dream that married couples would work together to build and not tear each other down. Not about doing things to be seen, but about allowing God to shine through them. It seems that with times in the past, more of the families that I saw worked harder together. As if they were in survival mode, so they were determined to make things work. I dream to continue to have the same tenacity with working with each other when the prosperity comes. Manage that along with the other things in the family.

I dream for more unity among the Christians in all that they are doing. That Sunday would not be the most segregated day of the week. That the church would have more of an impact on the government, school system, and business. In the past, the church had a bigger voice in education, politics, and the economy. More schedules were made around the church functions and activities. The things that the church would do caused others to take note and do the same. My dream would be for the church to be the model that others would want to follow. I would like the church to be able to take its rightful place.

I dream that the church would have a bigger voice and influence. That we would allow the church to be the backbone of the community as it once was in the past. That the church would be the place that people will look to get answers and not look to media and the news to give the understanding of things that are spiritual. That the church would have the bigger voice and influence with miracles, signs, and wonders following the word preached.

## FINAL WRAP UP

It would be good for us to look at the different ways that we can make God look better. What are things that we can do to give Him a great representation on the earth? Regardless of how things may change, you stay with God's Word and don't change. The customs and traditions of different cultures would be passed down from generation to generation. They remain the same and would not change or adapt to the climate or people that they are facing. When the culture changes, you continue to stay with God.

> Woe to those who call evil good, and good evil; Who put darkness for light, and light for darkness; Who put bitter for sweet, and sweet for bitter! Isaiah 5:20

The culture can change for different reasons. The opinions of the masses can change for different reasons. God does not change. He remains the same. Yesterday, today, and forever more.

In the last day of writing this letter, I was in search of a picture of some of my neighbors that lived on my block. In the process of searching, I found some letters from women that were trying to encourage me at a point in my life. I was a young teen off to school. I was hundreds of miles away and did not know anyone in the town where I moved. There were challenges in the school. Cultures were totally different from my own. I was not in a traditional college, so things operated in a different fashion.

The letters that I found were written by women who were mentioned in some of the stories in the chapters of this letter. Some were peers that graduated high school before me and some that graduated after me. Others were mothers in the neighborhoods where I grew up. They would call me their son. I did not understand everything that everyone wrote at the time. As I look back at what they wrote, I now have a better understanding and appreciation for them all. If you can only imagine. These letters are over 25 years old. I certainly appreciate the love and encouragement in a challenging time in my life. I pray that this <u>love letter</u> will be an encouragement to you. God Bless!

## INVITATION

An invitation was provided at the beginning of this letter. By taking the steps to invite Jesus in your heart, you will have a better understanding to the topics discussed in this letter. My prayer is that if you have not taken the steps, you do so now.

If you have in the past and have gotten away from God, I encourage you to recommit your life to Him once again. It would be a great thing for you and give you understanding as you read the content of this letter. There is no judgment here. I want to help you get your spiritual needs met.

## GIVE YOUR LIFE TO CHRIST.

> ...for all have sinned and fall short of the glory of God. (Romans 3:23)

> ...that if you confess with your mouth the Lord Jesus and believe in your heart that God has raised Him from the dead, you will be saved. For with the heart one believes unto righteousness, and with the mouth confession is made unto salvation. (Romans 10:9-10)

This can be done in prayer. Invite Jesus Christ into your heart. Believe that He is the Son of God and that God has raised Him from the dead. Confess Jesus Christ as Lord. Receive Him as Lord.

## SAY THIS PRAYER:

I am a sinner; I need a Savior. I need Jesus. I turn from sin, and I turn to You. I believe in my heart that You raised Jesus from the dead, and I ask Jesus now to come into my heart and be the Lord of my life. I receive Him now as Lord of my life, and I confess with my mouth that Jesus is Lord! Thank You for my salvation! In Jesus' name, amen.

## ACCORDING TO SCRIPTURE, YOU WILL HAVE A BETTER UNDERSTANDING OF GOD'S WORD.

> And He said, "To you it has been given to know the mysteries of the kingdom of God, but to the rest it is given in parables, that 'Seeing they may not see, And hearing they may not understand.'" (Luke 8:10)

## REDEDICATE YOUR LIFE BACK TO GOD

> If we confess our sins, He is faithful and just to forgive us our sins and to cleanse us from all unrighteousness. (1 John 1:9)

> ...far as the east is from the west, So far has He removed our transgressions from us. (Psalm 103:12)

## SAY THIS PRAYER:

Father, I have sinned, and I ask You to forgive me. I turn away from sin, and I receive Your forgiveness. I forgive myself. Now, I recommit my life to You afresh. I break the power of the devil over my life, in Jesus' name. Thank You, Father, for receiving me again, allowing me to have right standing with You. I confess that all my sins and transgressions have been removed.

## ABOUT THE AUTHOR

A native of Charlotte North Carolina. Born the youngest of three children Crawford grew up on the west side Charlotte. Even as westside resident Crawford attended schools in different parts of the city of Charlotte. He never wanted to live life through traditions or conforming to a mold that others would try to set him out to complete. Never remained on a path just because it was the popular route to take. Brought up in a Baptist church and did not develop a relationship with Christ until after high school. Did not develop a true relationship with God until he was off on his own away from home. The journey with Christ went from carnality to authentic with lessons learned along with the mentors, teachers and others that God has led to be part of his life. Works with different organizations to help win others to Christ. Crawford continues to serve in the helps ministry to serve others from different walks of life.

# RESOURCES

**Hebrews Streams**
http://www.hebrew-streams.org/works/ntstudies/yeshua-bar-abba.html
Yeshua bar Abba and Barabbas
By: Paul Sumner

*Businessballs.com 4/14/20*
https://www.businessballs.com/communication-skills/mehrabians-communication-theory-verbal-non-verbal-body-language/
https://www.bl.uk/people/albert-mehrabian

*What Every Man Wants in A Woman*
By John and Diana Hagee
*What Every Man Wants in A Woman*
*What Every Woman Wants in A Man,* pg 94.
*Charisma House, A Strang Company*

www.ingramcontent.com/pod-product-compliance
Lightning Source LLC
LaVergne TN
LVHW061036070526
838201LV00073B/5060